Suddenly Single

To Kerry
Always Live life to the
full

Suddenly
Single

by
Denise Chilton

Denise Chilton

Suddenly Single by Denise Chilton

Published by: Fernlea Publishing House

Books may be purchased by contacting the publisher and author at: www.denisechilton.co.uk

First Edition

Cover Design: Vanessa Randle
Typesetting and Page Design: Tanya Bäck
Copyeditor: Simone Graham

ISBN# 978-0-9957332-0-6

About the Author

Denise Chilton is an accomplished author, speaker, entrepreneur and life coach. She wrote the book, *Suddenly Single*, to help women overcome the heartbreak of an intimate relationship coming to an abrupt end. Denise writes from her own personal experiences and she also draws on hard learned lessons from a wide range of brave women she has coached over the years.

Denise specialises in the business of relationships. She worked for over 15 years in operational management in corporate banking in the UK before launching her own business. In 2010, she found her calling in coaching and became a certified Professional Co-Active Coach through the Coaches Training Institute. She has built a business working directly with women as an Executive Business and Life Coach supporting them in all aspects of their life and speaking to audiences of women about work-life balance and leadership.

In particular, she champions women business owners, senior women leaders in business and emerging leaders to be successful, confident and reach their full potential.

Her client base includes businesses of all sizes, from across the public, private and not-for-profit sectors in the UK and Europe.

Denise is a regular contributor to a number of local and national publications and radio. Denise lives in Cheshire, England.

Very Special Thanks

To the brave women who shared their stories: thank you for trusting me.

To the men who chose to come into my life and stay a while: thank you for what our time together taught me about myself.

To my writing mentor Sian-Elin Flint-Freel: thank you for holding my hand out of the starting blocks and championing me on.

To my editor and guru Simone Graham: thank you for sharing your expertise and wisdom and getting me over the finish line.

To my creative book cover designer Vanessa Randle: thank you for visualising my values and loving "the woman" as much as I do.

To my designer Tanya Back: thank you for patiently waiting in the wings with your magic wand and bringing it all together.

To my 4 o'clock in the morning friends; thank you to Anne, Barbara, Barbs, Carol, Jane, Mandy and Sue who stood in the chaos of the early days and told me it would be okay.

To all my other lovely friends who have come into my life over the past 14 years: thank you for believing in me, even when I didn't.

Thank you to you all for your love, support and inspiration and being simply fabulous!

Contents

Preface 10

Introduction 12
  Suddenly Single 12
  Who Is This Book For? 13
  How This Book Works 14
  Why Is It Important That You Read This Book? 15

Chapter 1: A Relationship on the Edge 17
  My Own Relationship Reflections 17
  Behind the Scenes 20
    Your Sixth Sense 20
    Recognising the Warning Signs...............................21
    The Big Ask 22
  The Rehearsal Space..24
    The Intuitive Way 24
    Find a Friend...25
    Ask Questions, Act Early..26

Chapter 2: Alone with Your Broken Heart 29
  Relationship Reflections by Sandra 29
  Behind the Scenes 31
    Getting To Grips with Grief....................................31
    Taking the Edge Off 33
    Just Say "No" 34
    Connecting with Others..35
    Being with the Pain 36
  The Rehearsal Space..37
    Appreciating What You Have 37
    Practical Steps to Self-Care 38
    Naming and Processing Your Emotions................39
    Your Aching Heart 40

Chapter 3: Keeping Up Appearances 42
  Relationship Reflections by Rosie 42
  Behind the Scenes 45
    Do Opinions Really Matter? 45
    Start Spreading the News 46
    Fair-weather Friends..47
    The Domino Effect...48
    Betraying Yourself 50

The Rehearsal Space...51
    What To Say and Who To Say It To 51
    Dealing with Disappointment 52
    A Little Inspiration..53

Chapter 4: The Practicalities of Single Life.................55
My Own Relationship Reflections 55
Behind the Scenes 58
    We Can Fix It!..58
    The Financial Forecast...59
    First Time for Everything..61
The Rehearsal Space...62
    Do What You Love..62
    Money Talks 63
    Do It Yourself SOS...65

Chapter 5: Return of the Ex.......................................67
Relationship Reflections by Lisa.......................................67
Behind the Scenes 70
    Back For Good? 70
    Affairs of the Heart..71
    Is it Really Over?..72
    Life in the Other Camp 73
    No Commitment, No Success......................................75
    Are You Ready To Forgive? 76
The Rehearsal Space 78
    Questions, Questions, Questions 78
    Learning to Trust Again 78

Chapter 6: Processing the Loss of Your Happily Ever After 81
Relationship Reflections by Sarah.....................................81
Behind the Scenes 84
    The Shame of It All...84
    Not So Happily Ever After...84
    Make the Change - Manage the Transition................85
    Endings and Letting Go...86
    Entering the Neutral Zone 88
    A New Beginning 89
The Rehearsal Space...90
    The Closing Ceremony 90
    Releasing the Remnants 91

Chapter 7: Discovering Your True New Self 93
Relationship Reflections by Rebecca 93
Behind the Scenes 96
    A New Beginning for the New You..............................96

A Relationship with Yourself 96
Valuing Your Values 97
Do Something Daring 99
Step Away From Your Comfort Zone 100
Feel the Fear and Do It Anyway 102
The Rehearsal Space..103
Where Am I Now? 103
What is Most Important? 104
The Best Intentions 106

Chapter 8: The Dating Game... 108
Relationship Reflections by Deborah.................................108
Behind the Scenes 111
The Dating Game 111
Question Time..114
The Single Search...115
When the Whistle Blows 116
It's Just Emotion That's Taking Me Over 118
The Rehearsal Space..118
The Right Match 118
Fact or Fiction? 119
"Date Night" with a Difference..121

Chapter 9: The Last Married Man.................................. 122
Relationship Reflections by Annie.....................................122
Behind the Scenes 126
Four Stages of Dating...126
The Heart Protector 127
Like Attracts Like 129
Know Your Limits 131
The Rehearsal Space..133
Risk Assess Your Relationships..133
Unhooking Yourself From an Unavailable........................134
The Right Relationship for the New You...........................135

Chapter 10: Stronger, Smarter and Simply Fabulous 136
My Own Relationship Reflections 136
Behind the Scenes 138
Taking Responsibility 138
Shared Learning of the Suddenly Singles..........................139
And Finally...141

Preface

"All great change is preceded by chaos."
- Deepak Chopra

The front door closed shut and I was alone. I sat on the sofa and curled up trying to stop the pain that was rushing through my body. "This is not really happening to me," I kept telling myself but the cold reality was that it was happening to me. I had seen the train coming down the track now for some time but had no idea how to stop it. That Saturday afternoon on a cold December day I had entered the world of the *suddenly single*.

This book is dedicated to the many women, who like me, at some point in their life have found themselves *suddenly single*. Who have woken up one day and found that their once familiar landscape which they had shared with a special someone had now dramatically changed and everything looked very different. For some of them, their partner or husband had exited stage left to find love elsewhere, for other women a courageous choice to escape from a relationship that no longer worked. Whatever route had got them to this place, it wasn't always one that they had chosen or felt they had control over. Now left feeling exposed, in an alien world, with a wounded heart that needed some serious mending, they needed some clues as to how on earth to navigate through this new land where all the rules had changed.

Shared reflections of women who have ventured through the land of "one" laughed and cried, messed up and got themselves back up. Have put the pieces of their heart back together again and along the way learnt some great strategies for experiencing life to the full and being whole again.

This has been written for you, with love and the message that you are not alone. What you went through or are still going through is part of the ebb and flow of life, the highs and lows, the bitter and the sweet. This book is in celebration of your courage and resilience and a knowing that you are enough.

Introduction

*"There are no wrong turns,
only unexpected paths."*
- Mark Nepo

SUDDENLY SINGLE

The 40 candles that had adorned the cake to celebrate my milestone birthday were scarcely cool. The birthday gifts still lay scattered around the house. The cards from family and friends wishing me happy times ahead were still on display. The new diamond engagement ring that sparkled on the third finger of my left hand was a reminder of the commitment we had just made to each other.

Six weeks later, seven simple words were to tip my world upside down, when the man I had lived with for the past five years and with whom I had planned my happy ever after, uttered "I don't think I love you anymore."

That one sentence was the prelude to what was to become my *suddenly single* journey.

I had thought that life was supposed to begin at 40 not fall apart. What I realised much later was that life actually had just begun. It was a very different life to the one I had envisaged but one where I would find out who I really was and what I was capable of.

The painful ending was the start of a new beginning. I was about to discover that the most important relationship in life is not the one you have with someone else but the one you have with yourself.

WHO IS THIS BOOK FOR?

If you have picked up this book, you may be searching for some help to make sense of what you are experiencing as a *suddenly single*. It's likely that you have exhausted your friends' advice and spent hours searching for resources, guidance and explanations or maybe even a good psychic who can reassure you that there is a bright future ahead! Like many women, you have probably befriended the internet hoping to find answers: *"How to mend a broken heart?"* *"How to stop the pain?"* *"Will he come back?"* *"How can I ever trust anyone again?"*

"Am I going mad?" or maybe simply *"Help!"*

To the outside world, it may look as if you have healed and moved on. You tell people *"yes, I am just fine!"* but this couldn't be further from the truth because on the inside, you are frustrated, you feel stuck and you are struggling to accept your situation. You might feel frightened to let go. *What of?* You aren't even sure.

It doesn't matter where you are on your *suddenly single* journey, whether it has just happened and you are still in the early days or whether you are much further down the road this has been written with you in mind.

Inside this book, you are going to find a selection of real-life experiences from real women, including my own, who have walked a similar path and successfully made it through: women who can relate to how you are feeling and what you are going through; women who once thought that they had found their "forever" relationship only to find it was suddenly over. For some women they had been betrayed by their husband or partner and others simply realised they have been betraying themselves.

HOW THIS BOOK WORKS

Each chapter is in three parts. At the beginning of each chapter you will find a *Relationship Reflection* from a courageous woman who has shared some aspect of her *suddenly single* experience. Next, we will delve *Behind the Scenes* to help you make sense of your situation so you can understand what is going on. Towards the end of each chapter, in *The Rehearsal Space,* I invite you to practise some tried and tested techniques; intended to help you heal, discover more about yourself and keep you moving forward. You may like to have a notebook or journal to hand to capture your own reflections and thoughts as you go along.

Everybody's *suddenly single* experience is unique and the stories you read may be very different from your own reality but my guess is that there will be something in this book that will strike a chord. And, even though this book reflects the experiences of women, *suddenly single* can happen to anyone at any age, regardless of gender or sexual orientation. Suddenly single has no boundaries.

WHY IS IT IMPORTANT THAT YOU READ THIS BOOK?

When we find ourselves in that *suddenly single* place, we arrive at the start of a brand-new chapter in our life's journey. It is our story and we can choose the role we want to play from here onwards. We can choose the role of victim or we can choose to be the heroine.

This book is for those women who want to be the heroine and understand what is happening to them. They want to heal healthily and positively and take responsibility for putting the pieces of their own lives back together.

Sometimes the heroine inside us gets stuck; she loses her voice and wants to run away and hide. Sometimes she wakes up crying in the middle of the night. Sometimes she jumps into a relationship that isn't right for her to take away the pain of loneliness or simply, to be like everyone else. Sometimes it's easier to be emotionally unavailable rather than take a risk and let love in again. Sometimes she slips into that victim role simply because she doesn't understand what is happening to her.

This book is the book I would have wanted to accompany me as I stood in the early days of chaos and through the months and years that followed. We all want someone to hold our hand sometimes and tell us it will be okay and I hope that this book will do just that for *you*.

Since 2010 I have worked as an Executive, Business and Life Coach supporting women in all aspects of their lives; helping them to discover more about who they are, what they want and how they can get it; encouraging them to find their inner strength so they can do the things that they thought were impossible for them; to learn to love all of themselves exactly as they are; to know they never have to settle for just 'okay'; to acknowledge all their emotions and learn how to manage them; to live their life to the full without compromising who they are; and to embrace life, however it unfolds.

"The journey of a thousand miles
starts with the first step."
– Lao Tzu

You have taken your first by picking up this book. Do not worry if the destination isn't quite clear yet, just trust that you will get there step-by-step.

CHAPTER 1
A Relationship on the Edge

"Follow your instincts.
That is where true wisdom manifests itself."
- Oprah Winfrey

MY OWN RELATIONSHIP REFLECTIONS

The ticket for the annual charity ball had been left in the fruit bowl on the dining room table. I remember picking it up to see if there was a second one attached. There wasn't. It was a ticket for one. It was in that very moment that I started to feel that something wasn't quite right.

When I asked my partner John where my ticket was I was told that, this year, there was a group of new people in the office and if I went along I wouldn't know anyone. He didn't want me to get bored with all the "office talk". John and I had met five years before in that very same office so I was very familiar with the "office talk" he was referring to. I didn't understand. My head told me that his rationale was perfectly logical while, at the same time, it felt like an intruder alarm was going off deep in the pit of my stomach.

It was just a ticket in a fruit bowl; an invitation to a night out. So, *what was my problem?* Despite his explanation, my mind kept going over a long list of other possibilities as to why I hadn't been invited. No matter how much I tried to make sense of it, the uncomfortable feeling deep in the pit of my stomach refused to settle down.

In those weeks leading up to the charity ball, I started to notice a slight change in John's behaviour. Our conversations had a different tone and any talk about the future was brushed off with a casual, "let's wait and see". He seemed distant and snappy and he made no attempts to be affectionate. I put it down to his stressful job, even though he was the most laid-back man I had ever known.

Surely, it couldn't possibly have been anything else? In the five years John and I had been together, life was good and I had never been happier. I had just turned 40 and not long escaped the corporate world to set up my own consultancy business. We had set up home in a lovely, rural Cheshire village in the North West of England and our small terrace cottage only needed some roses around the front door to complete the country-living feel. John and I were living the dream!

What I was blissfully unaware of was that this dream was about to turn into a nightmare …

On the evening of the charity ball, which I didn't attend, I awoke in the early hours to find his side of the bed empty and I immediately felt that something wasn't right. He walked through the front door at 4 a.m. to find me sitting in the lounge, in my pyjamas, waiting for him. When I asked him where he had been until that hour, he told me that he had been driving colleagues home and he hadn't realised the time. I felt my intuition firmly prodding me but again, I chose to ignore it. I chose to believe him because even the thought of any other scenario was too painful.

For the next nine months, my internal alarm bell became my constant companion but I became an expert at ignoring it: when he was late getting home from the office because he was "at the gym", yet his gym kit would rarely make it into the laundry basket; when he was assigned to a new project at work that required some unusual overnight stays in other parts of the country; when a friend of mine mentioned that, once again, she had seen John having lunch in the restaurant at work in the company of an attractive and much younger female colleague.

When I look back now, there were clues everywhere. On the occasions that I did question something, he always came up with a perfectly reasonable answer which would reassure me that everything was fine, at least until the next time.

I asked him a couple of times if there was someone else. Each time, I was met with, *"How could you say that? Don't be so ridiculous"*. Still, I started to look for evidence. I was like a detective at a crime scene but I wasn't even sure that any crime had been committed. All I knew was that, when you know someone very well, you also know when they are lying to you.

I wondered if I was going mad. I found an article in a magazine about how to spot if your partner is having an affair. I could probably tick five of the "yes" boxes but the other five, I couldn't be sure of. It left me even more confused.

I confided in a couple of good friends. One told me I was being paranoid. She reminded me that, just a few months earlier, John had asked me to marry him. *"He wouldn't have done that if there had been someone else"*, she said. *"Maybe it's just a mid-life crisis?"* The other friend sat quietly and just listened. She assured me that, whatever happened, she would be there for me any time I needed to talk.

When he finally blurted out over dinner one evening that he didn't think he loved me anymore, it felt like time had stopped still. Even though I was half expecting it, the shock made me feel like I had been tossed into the ocean where I was now frantically treading water trying to get back to land.

He assured me there was no one else; he just didn't feel the same way about me anymore. The phone calls to our home telephone, which when I answered had the caller immediately put down the receiver without saying a word, must have been a wrong number. It was all in my suspicious imagination.

BEHIND THE SCENES

Your Sixth Sense

So, was it all in my imagination? What was really happening? What would have helped me to make sense of what I was experiencing and reassure me that I wasn't going mad?

Intuition is our sixth sense. It's something that we all have and we all experience it in different ways. It goes by different names: hunches, inner knowing, a gut feeling, or synchronistic happenings. We can all identify with the feeling, although it may not be something we totally trust or feel confident enough to act upon.

Like me, some people feel it as a sensation or a gentle nudge in their stomach. Others feel it in their heart area, like a throb. For other people, it's a thought suddenly entering their head. Intuition is not directly observable but its effects often are. You can't see the wind but you can still see its effect as it moves through the trees or blows the washing dry on a clothes line.

Intuition is always active within us; it is just a matter of becoming aware of it. It has no logic and it shows up in the strangest of ways. For example, maybe you haven't seen someone for a long time but they suddenly spring into your mind.

Then, the telephone rings and you answer it only to discover it's that very same person. There's also the time you were waiting for the numbers for the prize raffle to be announced and you had a sense that your ticket would be picked and it was.

Whilst it's important to listen to your intuition, it's equally important that you don't become attached to your own interpretation of what it means. In a relationship, I like to think of the role of intuition as an early warning signal; to bring your attention to something that has changed and needs a closer look. Simply put, you may see signs of a change in behaviour that doesn't make 100% sense to you. In my case, it was the single ticket in a fruit bowl which lead to my discovery that the person I loved, trusted and I believed was my "happy ever after" relationship was, in fact, about to leave me for someone else. In other situations, the same signs could have led to a totally different outcome. The signs may not be obvious or easy to spot immediately but if you feel that something is odd then you need to dig a little deeper for the truth.

Recognising the Warning Signs

Fiona was a 42-year-old mother of two who had been with her husband for 20 years. The signs that something wasn't quite right started to appear gradually, over what had been a difficult two-year period, so it was a little trickier to pinpoint exactly what was going on.

Fiona's husband had gone through some of his own life challenges, including the death of his mother and father. There were certain changes in his behaviour that Fiona thought were understandable in the given circumstances, yet still she had an unsettled feeling that there was something else going on.

If she had to pinpoint what was different, it really stemmed from the change in their conversations. He was critical, often commenting that they didn't seem to have anything in common anymore and he was worried by the lack of passion in the relationship. It wasn't a sex thing, though there wasn't much of that either. He also wondered what they would do when the children left home. Given their youngest daughter was only twelve and the empty nest syndrome was some time in the future, Fiona was puzzled.

He started to withdraw from any kind of conversation with her which she found frustrating. When she challenged him and asked whether he was having an affair with a work colleague, whose name he kept mentioning, he denied anything was going on. Twelve months later, she discovered he had been lying.

Unfortunately, intuition doesn't come complete with a crystal ball to predict the future or give you detailed reasons as to why it's trying to get your attention. Similarly, reading your horoscope or consulting a psychic won't provide you with the certainty you are craving.

Therefore, trying to figure out what is really going on becomes your main task any time you experience those intuitive nudges. With only limited information at hand, there is a risk that your imagination will spin its own interpretation of your experience and fill in the gaps with stories that only exist in your head.

It's easy for these stories to become quite catastrophic and conclude that your partner is having an affair, that you're going to be left alone and that your partner will take all your money leaving you homeless and so on. While this is how our minds often work, the reality is that you don't have all the details and the only way you are going to find out is to ask.

The Big Ask

In my case, when it came to asking John directly, I came unstuck. It sounded so simple. All I had to say was, "*Are you having an affair? Have you met someone else? Why do I feel like you are pushing me away?"*

For months I had a lot of questions but I often lacked the courage to ask them. I was scared that if I did ask them, then my deepest fears would come true. Upon reflection, I realised that I wasn't ready to hear the answers so I just kept putting it off, hoping everything would work out just fine.

I spoke to a good friend, one who had earned my trust and with whom I felt safe to share my concerns. I found it hugely beneficial to gain a different perspective, take a reality check and rehearse for the tricky conversation that I needed to have with John.

There were a number of "tricky conversations" over the months leading up to his eventual departure and although he provided me with some almost believable explanations, I still felt that the truth hadn't really surfaced in any of them.

When it comes to affairs of the heart, I wonder what it really is that causes those we love to keep the truth to themselves and leave us in the dark. Why is it possible for them to dream up the most amazing excuses for their actions, their whereabouts and their behaviour, when telling the truth would be so much simpler? If you ask anyone who has tried to exit a relationship why they felt the need to hide the truth, they will often admit that they didn't want to upset the other person. If only they realised that they already had! The reality is that being let down gently isn't actually helpful.

Despite being told *"I'm not in love with you anymore,"* the shock acted as a buffer and I just didn't believe it. I craved all of the details so I could make sense of what was happening. Looking back on it now, the kindest thing I could have done for myself was to give up "needing to know". Even if I had been given all the facts, it wouldn't have changed the basic truth: *he wasn't in love with me anymore.* It was hard to hear and even harder to accept but that was the truth of my situation.

I spent many months waiting for John to make a decision about our future together when actually, it was me who needed to make a decision about my *own* future. One day, after yet another unexplained night away, I arrived at what I came to call my "enough moment". It was a relief to hear myself finally say to him, "I would like you to move out."

There comes a time when you realise that sometimes no matter how much it hurts, walking away from someone you love has nothing to do with weakness and everything to do with strength.

THE REHEARSAL SPACE

The Intuitive Way

We are all intuitive. It's a natural biological function but if we have never had it explained to us, it can feel a bit odd! Intuition shows up differently for each person so it's important to learn to recognise when your own intuition is speaking and that you can trust what it says.

It feels like something that you can't quite put your finger on; you just know that something doesn't feel right. Imagine you have just walked into a room and two people have just had an argument. Even though you hadn't been party to their disagreement, you'll still likely to sense that something had gone on between them. That's your intuition.

A true sign of your intuition is when you get an unexpected or unsettled reaction during what appears to be a neutral or normal situation. Even though it can be scary to trust something you cannot see, be assured that your intuition is at work.

Here is a simple practice to help you to access your intuition. Read it through a couple of times and then do it as best you can from memory.

Find a quiet space to sit where you feel comfortable and where you won't be interrupted for about 10 minutes. Have your journal and something to write with close at hand.

Close your eyes and put your focus on to the tip of your nose. Become aware of your breath. For a few moments pay attention to the gentle rhythm of your breath going in and out. With each exhale, sink deeper into your internal world and let go of any outside thoughts. Know that you are in a safe and protected space.

Once you feel relaxed, pick one question that you want to ask of yourself about your current situation. You can think of your own question or try one of the questions below.

- *What wise words would I give myself about what I am sensing is happening in my relationship?*
- *What do I know for sure?*
- *What is the next step I need to take?*

In the quiet, just listen for your response. Take notice of any thoughts, words or images. Take out your journal and write anything that came to mind even if it doesn't seem to make sense. Spend a bit more time reflecting on what you have written and what you might need to do next. Learning to trust yourself will leave you in good stead for the path ahead.

find a friend

Asking for help can be incredibly hard to do when life is easy, let alone when you are in the face of turmoil, but it's important to have the right someone to confide in. It will help you keep perspective and ensure that you are taking the actions that are best for you. The good news is you probably know who this person is already.

Seek out someone who will listen, be empathetic and only give advice if it's asked for. Select someone who won't judge you and with whom you feel safe in the knowledge that they will keep your confidence no matter what. Talk to this someone today. Make a call, send an email or text. Let them know that you are asking for their help. You may not know what help you need exactly but simply reaching out is a positive step toward your own self-care.

While this person is likely to be very empathetic, just be mindful of their time and the level of commitment you need from them when you first reach out. If this person is a very close friend or family member, you don't necessarily want your problems to consume every waking minute of your time together. So perhaps you might agree between yourselves to some boundaries or give yourselves a limit of time as to how long you'll spend talking about your issues with them. If you really don't want to involve a friend, seek out the help of a life coach. They will have your total interests at heart and they can help you work through your emotions and show you how to develop a plan of action that is best for you whatever the circumstances.

Ask Questions, Act Early

When someone we love starts to behave out of character, it's a normal reaction to jump to all sorts of conclusions. No matter how much you think there is an affair going on, try to hold back on making accusations if you have no concrete evidence. Ask the question, stick to the facts and simply note the answer and the reaction. If you aren't convinced their responses are the full truth, then keep a note of what you are seeing until you get to a stage when you feel you have sufficient examples or evidence to be able to have an in-depth conversation.

If you feel like you are walking on eggshells in your own home then it's time to take action. If you don't speak up and you continue to pretend that it's not happening, you will continue to feel stuck and frustrated so prepare instead for a courageous conversation. Begin by writing down the questions and rehearsing what you want to say. If you have confided in a friend, run it past them or speak to your life coach. You don't have to learn it off by heart but having an idea of what you want to say will help you stay in control of the conversation, especially if your emotions try to take over. There will be questions that you may not want to hear the answers to but these are the questions that need to be asked the most!

Decide on a place to have the conversation. It may be somewhere in your home that you like to relax, it might be outdoors in the garden, or it may be in another place where you like to be together. In any case, choose a private place where you feel comfortable.

Tell him that you want to talk about some things that are concerning you and then say what you are noticing. The important thing is to stick to the facts. In my case, "*The night of the charity ball you didn't come home until 4 a.m. You have been working late a lot. You told me that you are stressed at work.*" Then explain the impact it's having on you. For me, "*I'm feeling unsettled. I feel on edge. I feel disrespected.*" I then asked him if there was anything else he wanted to tell me about the occasion or the recent circumstances. He didn't but at least I had asked.

If he is defensive and you feel you aren't getting anywhere then stop the conversation and agree to talk another time. It may take a few discussions like this over the coming weeks and months but keep it going and don't give up.

These conversations will empower you to get the information you need to make your own decisions and to help you start to moving things forward. Let go of any expectations of getting every detail. In most cases, you will have to make decisions without a fully clear picture of what is going on but by having the conversation, you have taken responsibility for yourself and the situation. Of this, you should be proud.

In the end, the best decisions are those that are made *using both your head and your heart*. It's not often possible to think beyond that first step so make the decision that is best for you, act on it and the rest you can work it out as you go!

CHAPTER 2
Alone with Your Broken Heart

*"Sometimes when things feel like they are
falling apart, they may be actually falling into place."*
– L.J. Vanier

RELATIONSHIP REFLECTIONS BY SANDRA

Let me just say that being told by my mother, *"You always did pick the wrong men,"* wasn't terribly helpful when I had just announced to her that my husband of three years had left me. Admittedly, I hadn't been terribly lucky in love in my 20s or 30s but when I met Tony in my early 40s, I thought it would be forever. He had been married twice before and I was hoping that his third time would be lucky for us both. Alas, it was not to be. Instead it looked like it would be his *fourth time* lucky, this time with a woman whom he had dated before he met me. I was devastated.

In those first few weeks after he moved out, everything looked the same. I was in the same house, with the same furniture and I travelled the same route to work. However, it *felt* very different. Each day I went through the motions; putting on a brave face to the world and declaring "*Yes, I'm fine,*" to anyone who asked. Inside, I was *anything* but. Some evenings I would pull the car up into the driveway and wonder how I had even made it home. The silence in the house was deafening and I found myself putting on the TV or radio just for background noise. It was an attempt at distraction but turned out to be small comfort. No matter how loud I turned it up, it couldn't drown out the unhelpful thoughts and questions that continued to go around in my head as to why this had happened to me.

Before I knew it, I had lost two dress sizes. People told me I looked amazing. I managed to get into my first pair of skinny jeans since skinny jeans came into fashion. Was becoming *suddenly single* the secret to dramatic mid-life weight loss, I wondered?

However, that was about the only positive side-effect I got from the break-up. The emotional rollercoaster was very unpleasant. I had to deal with emotions I had never experienced before and they frightened not only me but also my friends. I started acting out of character, going into stalker-woman mode. It wasn't pretty. I was sending very nasty emails to my ex and his new woman. It was a way of unloading all the rage I felt inside. I had never been in a situation where I'd felt such anger. Writing out how I felt was the only way I knew how to manage it. Whilst putting it all in an email felt therapeutic, I actually felt a deep sense of shame after I pressed the "send" key.

Eventually, I reached out for help and asked a friend to step in to act as my voice of reason. Once I talked it through with her, I came to realise that it was important to have someone hear all of the raw 'stuff' I was feeling. I kept writing the emails but this time when I hit send, my friend became the new recipient. I was grateful to her for agreeing to be the one I could vent to. Eventually the anger started to dissolve and I took up journaling each day as a more helpful strategy to manage my thoughts and feelings.

Going to bed each night alone and waking up alone were other reminders of my new status. For the first few seconds when I opened my eyes in the morning, everything seemed normal and then suddenly, I'd remember what had happened and that sinking feeling in my stomach returned. No matter what time I went to bed, 3 a.m. became my new waking up time. I couldn't concentrate enough to read so I would lie there until the early hours crying myself back to sleep.

"One day you will wake up and it won't hurt anymore," I was told by a well-intentioned friend but I didn't want to wait until *one day,* I wanted it to stop hurting right now. I began to wonder, *do hearts really break?* I had what can only be described as a physical pain around my heart in my chest that would, at times, actually *ache.* Was there a medical explanation, I wondered? It felt like my heart had been shattered into a thousand pieces and it was now my job to put all the pieces back together like a huge jigsaw puzzle.

Whenever I was trying to find an answer to help me understand what I was experiencing, my first point of call was the internet. I discovered that US researchers had found that the heart of a person who has undergone a severe trauma can hurt in the same way as pangs of intense physical pain. The areas in the brain that become activated to physical pain are also activated when we experience intense stress. I felt like quite the scientist and the self-diagnosis helped me to conclude that I was normal.

BEHIND THE SCENES

Getting To Grips with Grief

After a relationship ends, it is normal to experience a range of emotions, some of which you may have never experienced before and like Sandra's story, you may well have reactions that seem to be completely out of character. The stages of grief that you may experience when mourning your broken relationship are not unlike that of recovering after the death of someone who was very dear to you.

Swiss psychiatrist, Elisabeth Kübler-Ross, introduced a model to help people understand the emotional stages experienced when dealing with a loss. Although this model originally related to how to process a reaction to a death, the Kübler-Ross model can be applied to the loss of a job, a home, a major rejection, or the ending of a relationship.

The five stages under this model are denial, anger, bargaining, depression and acceptance. People move through these different stages at various speeds and not always in the same order. When you are dealing with any major loss, you might sometimes feel that you're moving forward and then something happens to set you back or vice versa.

A few months after John and I separated, I noticed I still had a lot of unanswered *"why?"* questions and found myself often contemplating *"if only..."* which indicated that I had made it through to the bargaining stage and I was still of the mindset that he would come to his senses and return. When he paid me a visit to pick up the last of his belongings, he announced that he had met someone else. They had been friends for some time. Still he was quick to assure me that they had only started having a relationship *after* he had left me. I wondered which part of *that story* he thought I would believe. I sarcastically asked him what he thought his new, younger girlfriend was hoping to gain from a relationship with a man 18 years her senior. He had no answer.

Surprisingly, my overall reaction to his news was relief. After all those months trying to figure out what my intuition had been trying to tell me, I finally had my suspicions confirmed.

When I thanked him for letting me know, he looked at me in astonishment.

It was much later, when I had time to process what I had heard, that the fury set in. It felt like I was sliding backwards. If he had told me the truth when I had first asked him if there was someone else, then I would have been much further along in the healing process.

Taking the Edge Off

As human beings, we are designed to give and receive love. It's a basic human need. We need it in the same way we need food, water, shelter and security. If we don't attend to our basic needs, there can be a damaging effect on our physical and emotional health. When we don't have water, we get thirsty. When we don't have enough food, we get hungry. When we experience the break-up of a relationship, it leaves us with an emptiness that exposes our basic need for love.

For many people the easiest way to deal with the pain is to take the edge off. Numbing the pain comes in many guises: maxing out the credit card, comfort eating, drinking too much wine, or even jumping into a new relationship. These things provide temporary relief but the after-effects are likely to leave you with even bigger problems than the pain in your heart.

There's no such thing as a quick fix for a broken heart. Think of it this way, if you went to hospital for an operation and the surgeon rushed through, put a dressing over the deep open wound but forgot the stitches, it might look okay for a short while but eventually the dressing would come away and expose the open wound. In the same way, the heart cannot be hurried through the healing process.

The best place to start your healing journey is by learning to love yourself. It may seem cliché and a rather uncomfortable practice, particularly if you are an expert at putting other people's needs before your own. Attending to your own self-care might feel selfish but if you don't care for yourself then you won't be able to care for others who might be relying on you. When you start to realise that you are good enough just as you are, love from another person becomes a bonus, rather than a benchmark, for your self-worth.

So do you treat yourself like you would your best friend? Do you talk to yourself with kindness and empathy? Or are the conversations you have with yourself full of blame, guilt and unreasonably high expectations? Self-love means you put your own needs first and reassure yourself that you are doing the best you can. It can take a lot of practice.

Just Say "No"

Tina was a striking, thirty-something, single mum of twin daughters. She had been the main organiser of an annual fund-raising event at her daughters' school for the last five years, where she was on the Parent Teachers Association. It was a big commitment that took up a lot of her spare time and involved numerous meetings and endless phone calls to make sure it all ran smoothly.

Within a couple of months of her break-up, the time came for the first planning event. Her heart told her to throw herself in and get on with the job but her head told her she needed to be around for her girls. As much as she hated to admit it to herself she also knew she didn't have either the physical or mental capacity to take charge of this year's event. When she asked one of the other Mums to take over her duties, so she could step down to take on a much smaller role behind the scenes, she initially felt terribly guilty. Yet she knew that if she didn't ask for help, the person she would be letting down most would have been herself.

It takes courage to say "no" to things when you feel there is an expectation on you but if you don't have the energy to take on a commitment, it's perfectly acceptable to give yourself permission to hand the reins to someone who can.

Connecting with Others

There will be times when you'll want to hide away from the world. Be assured that it's a perfectly normal reaction when you're going through such stressful times of change.

However, connecting with others has its benefits, especially in the early days, when you may be feeling more vulnerable than usual. Making sure that you are connecting with the right others is essential. You want people around you who are supportive and who will make you feel better, not those who are enjoying your drama and making you feel ten times worse.

For me, I found that having some regular daily interactions helped keep the negative thoughts at bay. At the time of my break-up, I was working for myself which meant I was living alone and working from home. If I didn't plan anything, then I might not see anyone for a couple of days at a time. Being home alone for days, with only the cat for company, was not an environment that served me well. Instead, I made a habit to take a lunch break and go to the local coffee shop on the days when I was home alone. I would also make time to meet someone or at least chat on the phone; to help me stay connected to the outside world.

Being on your own can become *too comfortable*. It's easy to retreat and cut yourself off completely and you might not notice at first how isolation can impact your mood. Keep your eye on the balance. There is a big difference between *being alone and hiding away*.

Having friends or someone you can reach out to is essential

during the early months. I was fortunate to have a few friends that heard my raw stuff but not all your friends will be willing to do that. Different friends can be valuable in various ways so only unload to those for whom it won't be a struggle.

Being with the Pain

Just like Sandra, I too wanted to believe that I would wake up *one day* and not feel the pain. I was hoping that someone would invent a big fast-forward button that, when pressed, would take me far into the future so I could skip the heartache and have my life return to normal; whatever normal was. It wasn't until much later in my own healing process that I realised that the heartache is an essential part of healing from this kind of loss.

When we have tried every avoidance tactic in the book and the pain still doesn't go away, then the most effective way to deal with it is to acknowledge its existence. Denial and suppression of emotions is unhealthy. Sadness needs to flow through the body and then be released. If it doesn't get processed properly, it gets trapped inside our bodies; sometimes for years, causing not only emotional pain but also damaging our physical health.

Our natural reaction to pain is to wince and try to ignore it but it's healthier to stop fighting against it and spend some time becoming familiar with it. When we do, it loses its power over us.

I found it interesting to learn that tears can actually help facilitate the flow of sorrow through our bodies so we can release sadness more easily so if you need to cry, then don't hold back. Let it flow and feel the sorrow. Remember it's just an emotion and each tear shed is one step further in your healing process.

There is no magic cure to make what you are going through go away overnight. However, dealing with your vulnerabilities, recognising that you have a wound, learning to put yourself and your own needs first and simply being with and acknowledging the painful emotions are all effective ways to help your healing process.

Keep going. Each step may feel like it's getting harder but don't stop. Even the smallest actions can be steps in the right direction.

THE REHEARSAL SPACE

Appreciating What You Have

Practising gratitude on a daily basis and bringing your attention to the things that you have in your life, rather than what you are missing, can help you feel more positive. This might seem impossible to comprehend especially if you are feeling that your life is in tatters and you are experiencing high feelings of frustration, anger and loss. However, when you appreciate the everyday things around you, that you sometimes take for granted, it helps to give you a different perspective on your situation.

Here is an easy way to start. At the end of each day, pick three things that you are thankful for and write them down in your journal. It could be a walk in the park, clean sheets on the bed, or sunshine shining through the window. Appreciating what you have, rather than what you don't, does make you feel more positive and can help keep the negative self-talk at bay.

On my gratitude list was a bed to sleep in, a roof over my head and the friend who gave me an hour of her time. On the days when I struggled, I reminded myself to be thankful even for the struggles because the pain in my heart reminded me that I was alive.

Practical Steps to Self-Care

Attending to your own self-care needs may not be high up on your priority list but it's very important to find ways to invest in your well-being. Start by making a list of things that make you feel nice or that you enjoy doing. These can be simple everyday things. Start with five of them, then challenge yourself to list five more. Aim to have a list of 20 or 25 things so you have lots of options.

Then each day select at least one thing to do, just for yourself. If it's a particularly tough day, then do a few. Give yourself permission to think of nothing but what you are doing and be totally present so you can enjoy each moment. If you are going for a walk, then focus on what is around you. Take in the nature, the birds that are singing, the noises you hear and the scents that are in the air. If you are dancing around the house, do it like no one is watching.

Here are some suggestions to get you started.

- Take a warm bath with bubbles and scented candles.
- Meet a friend for coffee.
- Put clean sheets on the bed and have an early night.
- Make a telephone call to someone you have been meaning to call.
- If you wake in the middle of the night and can't sleep, then make a cup of tea and sit in the middle of the bed with the lights full on, just because you can!
- Go for a bike ride.
- Lay on the grass staring up at the sky and do some cloud watching.
- Cook a nutritional meal that will feed your body.
- Journal your thoughts and feelings in a special notebook.
- Go out for the day to the coast or the mountains to get a

change of scenery.
- Make yourself a *suddenly single* playlist of your favourite tunes.
- Listen to your playlist and dance, dance, dance.
- Schedule personal time every day for yourself.
- Have your hair done.
- Buy yourself some flowers.
- Have a manicure.
- Bake a cake just for you.
- Take a lunch break.
- Burn a scented candle and make a wish as you light it.
- Watch a good movie.
- Have a massage.
- Do something physically active that you really enjoy.
- Say "no" to a commitment when you would normally say "yes".
- Dress the way that you want to feel.
- Ask someone to do something for you.

Naming and Processing Your Emotions

It's perfectly acceptable to feel angry, furious, mad, or sad. Anger is a result of feelings that have not been communicated and have built up inside us. Ultimately, they will explode; pushing anger away and refusing to deal with it does you more harm than good. So admit to yourself that you are angry and put a name to the emotion. When you put a name to it, your brain can then make sense of what is happening to you and it starts to settle down.

Take a moment now to think about how you are feeling about your situation and name the emotion. Write it down in your journal. "I feel angry. I feel sad. I feel disappointed. I feel lonely". Acknowledging the way you feel, is the first step to dealing with it. If you are feeling particularly emotional, then keep writing until you feel you have expressed what you need to say. It's much better out than in.

Writing in a journal is like having your own secret diary and this can be a very helpful way to express and process your emotions about what you are experiencing. Make it a regular practice. Pick a time of the day that suits you best and spend just 15 minutes writing down what you are feeling and thinking. There are no rules, so write whatever comes to mind. If you have no words, then draw pictures. It doesn't have to make sense to anyone else, only to you. Then reflect on what you have written or recorded on the pages and think about what you are learning.

Your Aching Heart

When you are at the eye of a tornado of emotions, you may experience physical pangs of heartache. Stepping into that place of pain will help you understand what you are feeling so you can stop being afraid of it.

Start by finding a quiet space to sit where you feel comfortable and won't be interrupted for at least ten minutes. Have your journal and pen to hand. Close your eyes and put your focus on the space around your heart. Think about the "ache" you feel.

- What kind of ache is it?
- Is there anything else about that ache?
- When does the ache appear? What are you doing? Who are you with?
- What happens just before you notice the ache?
- If it was a size and shape, what would that be?
- What does that ache need right now, in this moment?

Heartache may never be your best friend but if you ac-knowledge that it exists then you can see that it's simply an emotion. It will no longer be something to fear or hold you back.

CHAPTER 3
Keeping Up Appearances

"When you come out the storm, you won't be the same person who walked in. That is what the storm is all about."
- Haruki Murakami

RELATIONSHIP REFLECTIONS BY ROSIE

As tempting as it was, I quickly realised that posting a message on Facebook and changing my relationship status to "single" probably wasn't the best way to let my friends and family know that my husband had left me, though it crossed my mind that it would have been an easy way out.

I struggled to understand it myself and just knowing that I had to explain it to someone else too felt really overwhelming. My husband's sudden departure meant I was left to spread the news that we were no longer a couple, an undertaking that I felt was very unfair. After all, it had been his decision to leave me and yet here I was, responsible for telling our friends and family.

I wondered what I was supposed to say. That my husband and I had separated? That he had left me? Should I say he had left me for *someone else*? How much did people already know? What if everyone already knew of his affair? If that was the case, maybe I was the last to know? I felt so ashamed at the thought.

I came to dread taking my son to football practice on a Saturday morning. I would stand at the side of the pitch with the other parents exchanging pleasantries. I was waiting for someone to ask me a question about my situation but the reality was that no one said a word. I wondered "*do they know?*" Maybe they felt too embarrassed or even worse, they didn't really care.

When it came to telling my family and close friends, I noticed that I put my own feelings aside and almost made light of it. It was still only early days and I was in denial, hoping my husband would realise the error of his ways and come back to me. If I could just stop people from judging him, then they wouldn't feel embarrassed and regret what they had said, should there be a reconciliation.

I wasn't sure why I was protecting him and his reputation after he had caused me so much hurt. Nevertheless, I became quite the performer; holding the tears back and controlling the wobble in my voice as I did my best to soften the blow for our family and friends. I couldn't keep up the façade for very long because people were sad to hear my news. I was so busy trying to deal with my own loss, I hadn't even thought about the impact my *suddenly single* status might have on them.

My husband had been a part of our family for 22 years; since our college days. Regardless of the circumstances of his very quick departure with someone else, when the dust settled, he was still missed. My brother likened it to losing a very good friend whom he had not had a chance to say goodbye to.

Close friends of mine were very supportive. I came to affectionately call them my "4 o'clock in the morning friends". No judgement and no advice-giving (unless asked for). They simply listened. They would have been there at any time of the day or night, should I have needed it. I felt very reassured to know that they were there, just in case.

The break-up brought me closer to some people who I wouldn't have called "close friends" beforehand, but they had been through a similar journey. I found that the shared experience made me feel less alone and as miserable as I felt, I also came to appreciate that I was more fortunate in some ways than other people.

Friends that we had made as a couple didn't always react as I would have expected. "*What will we do at New Year now?*" said one of my husband's friends rather clumsily. For the past five years, we had welcomed the New Year in with two other couples and their children. Since this was only April, I put his thoughtless comment down to shock and I did my best to put my hurt to one side.

Quite a few people insisted they didn't want to take sides but I knew some felt compromised. It was inevitable, I guess, that there would be a natural divide. A few months later, when one couple had a summer BBQ and they invited my husband and his new girlfriend but not me, I was incredibly hurt. They were more his friends and less mine but we had gone on holiday with them and had many years of shared memories and good times. It was awful but it was something I was to become used to in my strange new world.

It wasn't just the humans going through the loss. Bernard had been the family cat and we had welcomed him into our house when our son was younger. He was a real explorer and would often disappear for days at a time, only to be brought home by a thoughtful neighbour who had rescued him from a garden shed or from behind a locked door.

When my son was out at his friends and I was home alone, Bernard was very good company, serving as an anchor to my old world. Each evening at 6 p.m. he would wait by the front door, listening for the familiar sound of my husband's car engine pulling up outside which signalled, in his world, that someone who loved him was about to walk through the door and make a big fuss of him. When the car didn't show up, he would walk back into the living room and sit staring up at me with a puzzled look on his face, as if to say, "*where is he?*" It was quite evident that Bernard was grieving too and struggling with the new landscape.

It seemed that I wasn't the only one wishing for a time in the future when life would feel familiar again.

BEHIND THE SCENES

Do Opinions Really Matter?

Dealing with a disappointment or failure of any kind brings on one of our biggest fears; what will people think about us. This is usually accompanied by a deep sense of shame. We may say we don't care but other people's opinions can make us feel judged or criticised, particularly when they are the individuals whose opinions we really do value.

When 32-year-old freelance writer Kate and her partner of six years agreed to go their separate ways after experiencing "irreconcilable differences", her father told her that he wasn't at all surprised because he hadn't expected their relationship to last more than six months. He then went on to say that he had never really liked her partner. Kate was dumbfounded that, for the past six years, she did not have a clue that her father held that opinion of someone she loved and cared about. He had never uttered a word. What else did he think and wasn't saying? Did everyone else think the same?

The sooner you can stop worrying about what people will think about you and your situation, the better. I remember someone telling me what people thought about me was none of my business, in the same way that *what* I thought of them was none of their concern either. This was a sombre thought but I have come to accept that it's absolutely true.

Start Spreading the News

When it comes to telling people your news, you may wonder where on earth to start. An outburst on social media may seem like a good way to get your side of the story out there, but hanging your dirty laundry up for all to see will only add fuel to the fire and the turn on the rumour mill, which is likely to leave you with an even bigger hangover of shame. Is it worth putting yourself through that?

Be cautious about what you choose to share and who you choose to share it with. You may want to tell your close friends and family and of course, that makes sense. They will want to offer support, however you don't need to tell them every detail. Only tell them what you want them to know.

When we are experiencing a difficult time such as a break-up, there can be a natural tendency to overshare. In the short term, you might feel that spilling out everything you know to anyone who will listen will make you feel better, but it probably won't do you any favours in the long run. Does the postman, your neighbour and the whole of the marketing department at work really need to know all the ins-and-outs of your tale of woe? Probably not.

Instead tell people on a need-to-know basis; only tell them the details you wish to share and stick to the facts. If you are making assumptions, you should say that you are making that part of the story up. People are going to quote you anyway and then add their interpretation on to what you have told them so be as factual as you can to reduce any damage.

No matter how much care you take to relay the facts as you understand them, things can still become mixed up and sometimes with catastrophic consequences. Shortly after John left me, I was interviewed by a national newspaper about my new consultancy business. The journalist learned I was recently single and asked me some questions about my break-up which I refused to answer as it had nothing to do with my business. I thought I had managed well by saying only a few carefully chosen words.

When the article was published, I was shocked to see that the journalist had made up parts of the story where I had left blanks. It gave the impression that my partner had left me in the early days of my new business venture and taken all of my money, leaving me close to bankruptcy. It was totally fabricated and left us both feeling hugely humiliated.

Fair-weather Friends

Friends will react in all sorts of ways. Some will be like Rosie's 4 o'clock in the morning friends; generous with their time and be more than happy to offer any support you may need.

Then there will be other friends who may not have your concerns as a priority and may well be dealing with traumas of their own. Louise was my high school friend and we had shared many youthful adventures. Unhappily married for many years, she met someone at work and started an affair at around the same time I became *suddenly single*. She used to telephone me to discuss her dilemma; sharing all the details of her clandestine meetings and secret rendezvous.

It was torture to hear the intimate details and it ignited my imagination with all sorts of additional scenarios that caused me to wonder if John had also done similar things behind my back. Louise was seemingly unaware of the impact this was having on me and it put a strain on our friendship. As much as I tried to stay friends, I finally had to ask her to stop confiding in me. She mistook my request as disapproval and the friendship didn't survive. It was another sad goodbye with someone who I thought of as a lifetime friend.

It can be challenging to have to deal with friends of yours who, as a result of your relationship, are now also close friends with your partner. The same is true for friends you made during your time as a couple. There isn't a handbook to guide them on the right thing to say or do. If the friendship had its origins with your ex, then that person may have already heard in confidence that the break-up was coming and you can see why that would feel especially awkward. You may not be included every time one of these people plans a dinner party, weekend break, or just evening drinks at the pub. It's not necessarily a deliberate attempt to upset you; it just may not be where their loyalty lies.

The Domino Effect

Whenever one couple breaks up, it can have a ripple effect on other couples close to them. Jane and her husband had been part of the local village community since their marriage 15 years ago. When her husband left her for a neighbour, she felt ostracised by the other couples in her social circle. She noticed that some of her women friends suddenly became less available to meet for a coffee or an impromptu drink. Jane felt that a few of them had become quite unsettled by the split and were concerned that their husbands might re-evaluate their own relationships and follow a similar path. It was obvious at times that some of her so-called friends didn't want her included anymore in group events because they thought she may hit on their husbands. Jane was astounded and wondered had they *seen* their husbands?

One evening, her two teenage girls came in from netball practice and announced that all the families of their teammates were going on a camping weekend. There was no invitation for them, they hadn't been included. She wondered who had made the assumption that they wouldn't want to go. They were still a family so what had changed? However, it seemed to other people that *everything had* changed. She wondered if it would have been better if her husband had died, rather than abandoned her. In that situation, there would have been a funeral with lots of flowers and cards to mourn her loss. People would have come to visit her, wanting to pay their respects and offering to help out in any way they could. Instead, there was absolutely nothing.

The reality is that some friendships will grow stronger, some will stay the same and some may not survive. If you really want to save certain friendships which are very valuable to you, then it may require you to take the lead and make suggestions to do things together. In other situations a simple acknowledgment that you know this is probably difficult for them too and an honest conversation to address any assumptions that either of you have might be all that you need to do. Putting things into perspective and taking another view of it all can sometimes be a huge help.

There is a saying that some friends come into our lives for a reason, to help us through a difficulty. Some come for a season and it is our role to offer support to them. Other friends are with us for a lifetime and we learn a whole lifetime of lessons from each other. It may not be obvious which category each of your friendships belongs in but for those relationships which have run their course, try to be grateful for the times shared and lessons learned and accept that it's time for you both to move on.

Betraying Yourself

The break-up of a relationship is painful enough. If there has been a betrayal and your partner has left for someone else, it will be accompanied by a deeper pain and an intensity of emotions associated with loss. When you also feel that betrayal from your friendship groups, it can not only hurt you deeply but can be terribly isolating.

But what happens if the betrayal involves no other person? What if you are in a relationship where the only person you have betrayed is *yourself*?

Meet Jennifer. She was the eternal optimist. She had always been able to make most relationships work even long after they were over. She could always find another reason to give her relationship one more go and always put everyone else's feelings first rather than her own. She had known her husband Scott since her late teens. They had met at the start of university when someone that Jennifer had been madly in love with had ended their three-year relationship. It had been the classic rebound.

Despite her instincts indicating that Scott wasn't the right long-term partner for her, she ploughed on. Before she knew it, she was 13 years into her marriage with two children. Jennifer was exhausted at the effort involved in keeping up appearances to the outside world that she had a perfect family life when the truth was it was anything but *perfect*.

As her 14th wedding anniversary dawned and with her 38th birthday party a few months away, she couldn't betray herself any longer and made the decision that she was going to leave. It had come to the point when it was no longer gallant to soldier on.

It took a further two years before she took any action. Instead, waiting for the right time became her favourite excuse - waiting until after Christmas, after someone's birthday and before the children went back to school. The words finally came tumbling out after a petty disagreement and she told Scott the devastating news that for her, their marriage was over.

Sometimes our path to being single in later years starts many years earlier. We conform to getting engaged, married and having children to fit in, be accepted or because we don't like being on our own. It's far easier to keep telling yourself it will all work out in the end than face the upset that you will inevitably cause. Only it comes full circle. When we ignore that feeling inside ourselves that is letting us know a relationship doesn't feel right, we end up single again, in the very place that we have been trying to avoid.

Ending a relationship is never going to be easy but if you are the one that is initiating the exit you can chose to separate with love.

Be authentic and honest about how things are for you. Think compassionately and treat the other person with respect. Say sorry without feeling sorry, show empathy and acknowledge the hurt you may be causing. Most of all, take responsibility for your part in what you see as the breakdown to avoid blame. Allow the other person all the time they need to ask questions and say what they need to and be sensitive in your responses. Speaking your truth may hurt someone but telling a lie in order to make them smile, in the long term, is much worse.

THE REHEARSAL SPACE

What To Say and Who To Say It To

We may have no control over what people think about us, but we do have control about which details of our situation we choose to share and with whom we shall share them. There will be people you are very close to, such as family members and good friends and you will naturally want to let them know what has happened. These are the people you can trust and you can count on to respect the confidentiality of what you choose to share.

Then there will be those people who are not in your inner circle who don't need to know every detail but it may be beneficial for them to know that you are going through a challenging time. Think about your manager at work, the teacher at your children's school, or your next door neighbour. For these people, work out why they need to know and ask yourself how this may benefit you. Then work out what details you want to share and keep it factual. It can help to write it down and maybe practice saying it, especially if you are worried that you might overshare and give too many details.

It can be helpful to come up with a few practised phrases. *"My partner and I have separated so I may need to be flexible with my hours on Wednesdays to pick my children up,"* for example. They may ask for more details but just keep to your script. There is no need to share any further information than what you are comfortable saying at that time.

There will be people who might seem to have the best of intentions but they are looking to enjoy someone else's drama. They are likely to ask leading and cryptic questions in an attempt to satisfy their own curiosity. Remain polite and have some phrases to hand that will bring the conversation to a close. I find *"why do you ask?"* is an effective conversation stopper.

Dealing with Disappointment

The dynamics of any friendship can change when a couple splits up. If you are the partner who has been left, then you may assume that everyone will rush to take your side. When that doesn't happen you may get upset, take it personally, or put unnecessary strain on a friendship you hoped to keep.

Unrealistic expectations often lead to disappointment. Take some time now to look at your situation from the couple's perspectives. How do they see your situation? Where could they feel compromised? Don't expect them to get everything right all the time.

If they don't invite you to dinner or ask you to join them on a day out, try not to take it personally. Would you be deliberately thoughtless if the situation was reversed? It's normal to feel upset but you don't have to let the upset get in the way of your friendship. Talk the matter through with another friend who isn't involved so that you can begin to process your thoughts and feelings. Then, if you feel it would be good to have an honest conversation about the impact that those actions had on you, at least you can do so from a rational perspective.

Know that there is no place for passive aggressive behaviour in any friendship, so saying, "*it's okay*" when you clearly know it's not okay, won't do you any favours. You have a right to speak your truth.

It could be that you have to make the effort to arrange some of your own gatherings and events to invite people along to, rather than waiting for others who tread softly around you.

As time moves on, people will forget about what happened and move on with their own lives and priorities. You just might not be one of them so try not to take it personally and let things go. True friends will stand by you no matter what.

A Little Inspiration

If you have completed the second Rehearsal Space activity in the previous chapter, you will already have your own tips for self-care. Take some time now to revisit that list and to think about any more activities that you may like to add or try out. It is important that you keep this practice up so it becomes second nature.

One of the things on my own list that I found works particularly well was reading inspirational quotes. If you are active on social media then you can't miss them, they are everywhere. I was surprised at how easily I could always seem to find a quote or some words of wisdom that, regardless of my mood, provided me with some comfort.

Over the coming months, collect a selection of inspirational quotes that resonate with you. Make them visible on screensavers on your laptop and mobile phone, write them in your journal or on post-it-notes and keep them on view on your desk. This isn't an attempt at being Pollyanna but small doses of inspiration and motivation do act as a brief escape to help you cope better. Here are the words of an old proverb, to start you off. "No matter how long the winter, spring is sure to follow."

CHAPTER 4
The Practicalities of Single Life

"There is more inside you than you
dare to think."
- David R. Brower

MY OWN RELATIONSHIP REFLECTIONS

During those first few months of becoming single, I discovered that as well as emotional vulnerabilities, there were certain areas of life where the practicalities left me feeling very exposed.

I had never lived on my own before. I had left home and had lived with someone else before I met John. Although I was very independent and not at all phased about domestic chores or dealing with any of the financial matters of running a home, I realised that I had adopted the traditions in our relationship modelled by my parents. Cooking, cleaning and bed-making were not a problem. However, I didn't have the slightest interest in fixing a leak, painting and decorating, or putting up pictures. As far as I was concerned, it wasn't my department.

John had left behind the most amazing tool box with some pretty impressive looking components but I didn't have a clue what they were for or how to use them. Asking for help was never comfortable at the best of times and I was damned if I was going to look like a helpless female by sending out an SOS.

My first attempt at putting up a picture was exhausting. What type of screws do I need? What size? Why have I got three different size hammers? What do I line this up with and how do I make sure it's hung straight? And this was only the planning stage. I sat on the floor and stared into the tool box. I was hoping for one of those cartoon film moments when all the tools dance out of the box and miraculously everything gets done by magic. It didn't happen.

After a few attempts and a quick check on the internet, I managed to get the picture up straight and secure enough to stay on the wall. I was thrilled. DIY was never going to be my favourite pastime but learning a few tricks for emergencies would be helpful. I also sought out recommendations for a few reliable tradespeople; for the more ambitious domestic jobs, which made me feel more in control.

Money was another area that needed some careful planning. There had always been two monthly salaries coming in and we had lived a comfortable lifestyle. John had totally supported my decision to start my own business and in the early days as I got started, we agreed that we would rely on his salary while I was finding my feet.

After he left me, he kindly offered to continue to contribute to the household income. He knew my business was still in its infancy and I was working hard to build a client base but it was taking time. I interpreted his gesture as his way of assuaging his guilt for leaving me for someone else and this brought out my strong independent side. I didn't want his money. I was determined I could do this on my own.

A few months later, one of my main clients experienced some problems of her own and was forced to terminate our contract. I wondered if I had been hasty in my refusal of John's help. I didn't have enough money coming in to pay my bills. The financial forecast really was not good.

I knew that my priority was to find a way to secure my finances, if only for a few months to give me some peace of mind. Despite the "what will people think" gremlin making an appearance to remind me I had failed, I found the strength to reach out for help. I made a list of the people whom I thought might be able to assist me to get work. It got me into action and thankfully silenced the gremlin voice in my head.

When one of my contacts said he needed someone to run his office, I gratefully accepted. It wasn't the ideal role given my career path but I knew it would provide me with some respite while I worked out my "*what's next?*" I felt disappointed to put my business on hold for a while, but at the same time, it made me more determined to be back in business before too long.

As I started to adjust to single life, there were a number of new experiences I tried out. Each experience pushed me a little further out of my comfort zone and helped me feel better about myself and my new circumstances. When I couldn't find anyone to go to the cinema with one weekend, I decided to go on my own. "*It's just the same as taking yourself on a date*," said a friend.

Still, I was quite apprehensive beforehand. I imagined a cinema full of couples who would all be staring at me, feeling sorry for me and wondering why I was on my own. It was nonsense really. I reasoned with myself that I had never had a problem attending business conferences on my own and walking into a room full of strangers. At least in the cinema I wasn't required to talk to anyone and who would see me in the dark anyway? What was the worst thing that could happen?

When the credits rolled at the end of the film, I felt a small sense of achievement. This may seem like a somewhat insignificant step to others, but to me, it was a very significant one. It was the first of many different kinds of solo outings which I was to enjoy in my new world.

BEHIND THE SCENES

We Can Fix It!

Finding yourself living alone can bring about a number of practical challenges, that you never even thought about when you were in your cosy couple world. A little bit of DIY may be therapeutic to one person but to someone else, just thinking about the hassle of getting something fixed can be a cause for concern.

If you aren't a practical sort of person or good with tools of any kind, then don't hesitate to find people who are. If you love making cakes and your friend likes tiling and grouting, then do a swap. If you're open to having a go at some basic DIY but you aren't too confident, then get someone to show you how or find a course.

If you do opt to hire a tradesperson, always get a recommendation. I've lost count of the number of builders, plumbers and decorators who didn't seem to want to come out for those small jobs or who charged exorbitant fees for doing something which took all of 10 minutes.

One of the first large domestic jobs I needed to organise was getting a new central heating boiler. When a colleague recommended his boilerman friend Brian, I have to say that the picture I conjured up in my mind of him was nowhere near the reality when I opened the door. I was pleasantly surprised to find Brian was wearing designer clothing and his fingernails seemed far too clean for someone who claimed he spent every day fiddling with pipes. I hoped his boiler installation was reflective of his impeccable appearance and good sense of humour.

But after the installation, there were a few hiccups that required some minor adjustments. In the course of the next week, I had to make a number of phone calls to attempt to get him back. He assumed that I should be able to navigate my way around the newly installed boiler to tighten a specific fastener while he gave instructions over the phone. He was talking a language I knew nothing about and after trying to explain himself several times, he finally said sarcastically, *"You do know how to use a screwdriver, don't you?"* It didn't earn him any brownie points in my book. I wondered if I had been a man, would he have used the same line.

If you are DIY-challenged and want one less thing to worry about when it comes to home maintenance then having a list of dependable, tried and tested, tradespeople at the end of the telephone can give you the peace of mind you are looking for.

The Financial Forecast

The financial forecast as a *suddenly single* will be different for everyone. For some, money will be in very short supply but for others the picture will be a lot rosier. When our financial future is threatened in any way, it makes us feel insecure. We can get so wrapped up in "what if?" scenarios that we pile more anxiety on to ourselves and add to the already overloaded list of things to worry about. It isn't about the money itself but what the money provides. At its most fundamental level, money is what keeps us fed, watered and sheltered. It provides us with our basic needs so it's perfectly normal to have concerns.

Bev was a vivacious 38-year-old Senior Sales Manager and had worked for the same popular high street chain store for over 12 years. After her break-up, she found that, despite having only her own salary, she now had money left over at the end of each month. Her husband was an extravagant spender and during the 10 years they were together the joint account was regularly in overdraft. When they split up, she didn't have to compromise very much to still be able to afford the essentials.

When she called the utilities company to have her husband's name taken off the water bill, she ended up relaying the story of her husband's adultery to the very nice Customer Service Representative at the end of the telephone. He politely listened and then recommended a reduction in her monthly direct debit since she would not be using as much water as when they were a couple. Bev was delighted.

His next advice was to contact the Council offices and advise them that she was now living alone. As a "single occupancy" house it would qualify her for a further 25% reduction on her Council Tax. A further bonus for her bank account.

For other people, the financial reality is much bleaker. Susan was a caring and conscientious stay-at-home mother with two young children. She worked a few hours a week at the local primary school as a teaching assistant. It gave her a small income of her own while her husband pursued a successful career in the corporate world.

Apparently, that wasn't all he had been pursuing; he later announced that he was leaving her for someone else. Although he paid maintenance costs for the children, Susan had trouble making ends meet. She had to make drastic changes to her spending habits to cut costs. When he announced that she would have to sell the house and find somewhere smaller to live with the children, because he intended to buy a place of his own, she was devastated. It was yet more change to adjust to and another something she loved that she had to let go of.

First Time for Everything

When you are in a relationship, you remember all the lovely "firsts". The first time you met, the first date, the first night together, the first house together. As a *suddenly single*, there are some very different firsts: your first morning waking up alone and the first time you announce you have separated. If you have children, then there is the first weekend that they leave you to spend time with your ex.

Claire's first evening alone without her children was spent with a large glass of wine and an uninterrupted soak in the bath. On the Saturday, she took herself off for some retail therapy, or rather window shopping. Towards the end of the afternoon, she remembered thinking that she better get back home; only to suddenly remember *there was nothing to get back home for.*

She had mixed feelings about that. On the one hand, she was sad because she felt that no one needed her. On the other hand, there was something liberating about the new phenomenon of "me time", where she could do exactly as she pleased; something she never seemed to have when she was in her marriage.

It took many more weekends alone before Claire stopped feeling guilty about her "me time" and came to accept that this was all part of her new routine.

Many of her friends were married with children of their own and didn't have the luxury of dropping everything for a weekend meet-up so she had to plan well in advance if she wanted to meet them but over time, Claire felt more comfortable spending her "me time" alone.

Whatever your circumstances, having free time in your new life is one of the perks of being single, even if at first it might seem like an alien concept. If you are used to putting everyone else first, then it can be hard to give yourself permission to do something for yourself.

If you are single and sociable and you don't want your new normal to be a weekend of not seeing anyone then make sure you make the necessary arrangements and plan in advance. People will assume that because you are single you are busy and that is not always the case.

If friends aren't available then use your "me time" to attend a fitness class, invest time in a new hobby or anything that involves getting out and meeting new people; all further steps to invest in your wellbeing and help accelerate your healing process.

THE REHEARSAL SPACE

Do What You Love

When you invest time in learning something new or take up an activity that you haven't done for many years, it not only gives you renewed energy but it also creates an opportunity for you to meet new people outside your existing social circle.

The hardest part when you are looking to do something new is not deciding *what to do*, but taking the action to get started. We can all make decisions and it's easy to let excuses hijack us but if we don't go into action, nothing will change.

Make a list of five things that you love to do but keep putting off. Now pick one and commit to taking some action. For example, if you love to sing, find out if there is a choir in your local area that you could join and make contact with them today. If you want to study something new, find a course that sparks your interest and sign up for it.

Be prepared to overcome your own excuses. You can probably think of a number of reasons why it's not possible to do something you really want to. You may think that you don't have the time or the money, or you might worry, *"What will people think? I might not be any good at it."* Think of any reasons that are stopping you from taking action and write them down now. Then write down a list of all the reasons why it is a good idea to go into action. What will going into action give you?

Now, just do something. Send an email, make a telephone call, look up some places online and make contact.

When you have done this, take another action. Drive to the venue and check it out beforehand or attend the first class. If it helps, ask a friend to hold you accountable for your actions as a way of encouragement. The sooner you start developing new interests and moving out of your comfort zone, the more at ease you are going to be in your new world.

Money Talks

Dealing with changes in your financial circumstances is usually another area of re-adjustment. If you find yourself in a place of abundance and things change for the better, then appreciate your situation. If you find yourself in a place of scarcity, then here are some financial first-aid tips that can help to ease your situation.

Create your own personal survival budget. Make a list of all your monthly costs and financial obligations. List all the essentials such as household bills, regular loan payments and anything else that you are committed to. This will give you an amount of money you need to live off and that your income streams must cover.

If the money coming in is less than what is going out, look to see where you could negotiate a reduced monthly payment. Contact your utility provider and explain your situation. It could ease the pressure to consolidate your credit card or loans into one loan so ask the question. Remember this is only a temporary measure to help you manage.

Be sure to include in your list all the other spending you have, such as grocery shopping, running your car and gym memberships. See if there are any reductions you can make to these expenditures.

If you are still struggling, try looking at the small things you spend your money on every day and see whether you can redirect some of that spending to reduce your debts or other more important needs.

Keep a written list of your spends for one month and then review it. *What do you notice?* If you buy one coffee every day on your way to work the costs can be quite significant. What about the magazines that magically jump into your shopping trolley and yet you seldom have time to read? Is there anything else that you buy on impulse or from habit? Think about each item and make a choice about what you could stop or reduce.

Do keep the balance. Cutting down on impulse spending and redirecting that spending can help in the short term but you do need to have some pleasures in life, particularly with what you are experiencing.

Look for ways to increase your income. Taking on extra hours, getting a second job, or selling things that you no longer need are common ways to boost your income. Consider what extra work you can fit in and again remember to try and keep the balance.

Finally, if your ex-partner offers to help out in the short

term when you're really strapped for cash, then swallow your pride and graciously accept. Pride has no place when it comes to your own self-care and it won't pay the bills.

Do It Yourself SOS

If your home is your haven, then it's very important that you feel safe and secure. When it comes to the practicalities of household maintenance, decide if there are any areas where you feel particularly vulnerable. Having some strategies in place will keep you safe and keep your stress levels low.

Make sure you know where everything utilities-related are in the house. It sounds really basic but if you always left those responsibilities to your partner then it's normal to not know what to do. For example, if you have a leak, you need to know how to turn the water off. If the house alarm is triggered when the power supply is interrupted, you need to know how to turn it off and reset it. Keeping on top of routine servicing will help reduce high repair costs and is likely to result in fewer costly emergency repairs. You might also consider a simple addition to your home insurance policy that means you have access to a tradesperson 24/7 for emergencies.

Make a list of recommended tradespeople for routine maintenance and keep it in hand. Always, always, always get quotes in writing from any trades people, even the recommended ones, before they start the work. Don't be afraid to get two or three quotes to be sure you are getting good value and so you'll know in advance exactly what you will be required to pay. If your instincts tell you something sounds too good to be true, then it probably is.

If anything related to your car causes you the same allergic reaction as DIY, take out some breakdown coverage to keep you safe on the roads.

Whatever it is that might make you feel anxious, whether it's changing a tyre, or grouting the bathroom, have a plan and either learn how to do it yourself or know who to reach out to for help should you need it.

CHAPTER 5
Return of the Ex

> *"Nobody can give you wiser advice*
> *than yourself."*
> *- Cicero*

RELATIONSHIP REFLECTIONS BY LISA

"I want to come back. I miss you and the children." How I had longed to hear those words in the early days just after Paul had left us! The moment I had dreamed of was finally happening and yet the euphoric feeling I had imagined in my mind was replaced by stunned confusion.

Here he was, sitting on what had once been *our* sofa, drinking coffee from his *usual* cup, as if nothing had happened. I lost count of the amount of times he uttered, *"I am so sorry."* I didn't know what to say. It had been six months since he had left. I was starting to settle into a new routine and find a new normal and so were the children. It was surreal.

As much as my heart wanted to rush in and shout *"yes,"* my instinct told me to wait. Unfortunately, patience had never been my best friend so by the time he had sipped the last of his coffee, my heart had overruled my head and I agreed to try again. Perhaps I should have taken some time to think about it but in that moment, I worried that if I did, he might change his mind.

Over the following weeks things were good, especially when I allowed my mind to stop its constant questioning. *Was he going to stay?* Was he still in touch with my replacement and was their relationship actually over? Could we really make this work?

The children were delighted when we told them we were reconciling. Their only question was why he wasn't moving back home straight away and I didn't know how to explain that to them. I didn't want them to know that, deep down, a part of me was still angry and I wanted to punish him. I didn't want him to think he could waltz back in as if nothing had ever happened. He was disappointed about my reticence but he said he understood.

He joined us for dinner a few evenings each week. On the weekends, he came and spent time with the children and he slept in the guest room whenever the planned daytime activities overran. I insisted he fit in with some of the new routines that I had established with the children. I knew that made him feel a bit like a stranger in the home he had helped to create, but I thought it would be best.

I noticed that each time he left to drive back to his rented apartment, I felt like I was reliving the day he walked out on me. The evenings when he didn't come around brought out my insecurities. Was he really working late or was he still seeing *her*?

Paul seemed in a rush to get everything back to normal; the way it used to be. He wanted to face the music with my family and friends but I wasn't ready for anything so bold. I was aware now of what some of them really thought about him and I wasn't quite ready to take on their "*after all he has put you through*" concerns. So I only told a select few whom I knew would be supportive and would be thrilled for us. *So why wasn't I?*

We did make time to talk. We talked and talked. I caught myself constantly asking questions about the affair. I thought by getting more details I would understand why he had done it. He seemed reluctant to keep going over it. He helped fill in some gaps and I found it painful to listen to the details. The inconsistencies from the original stories he told me at the time of the break-up did nothing to help rebuild the trust.

He told me it was an affair that shouldn't have happened; he just got swept along. He made it sound very matter of fact, like he had little choice. If I hadn't found out about it and asked him to leave, he was certain that it would have fizzled out. I wondered why I was now seeming to get the blame. Was it my fault for throwing him out too early?

I wondered whether it was really possible to forgive and move on. How does someone rebuild trust again after an infidelity?

A couple of months later I agreed to let him move his things back in to the house. I just wanted it to be like it was, but it wasn't. Our eight-year marriage and the relationship we had created had been broken and I knew that if we were to have any chance of success we would have to create a new and different relationship. I don't think either of us had expected that to be the case.

Not once did I even ask myself what I wanted. I had put everyone else first and had rushed to accept him back hoping to make it all better and numb the pain of missing him. I discovered the pain of being with a man I no longer trusted was actually worse.

I suggested we seek some professional support, even if it was to help with the letting go. After a few sessions it became clear that we still had a mountain of work to do to rebuild our marriage. I found myself at yet another crossroads and tried to put it all in perspective. I loved my children and had thought I was doing right by them in attempting to reconcile but I knew I needed to do the right thing for me and reclaim my sense of self.

I wasn't prepared to risk putting in the hard work when there was a chance he might do it again. My children would be just as loved, have a home life that was stable and they would be okay, even if their father didn't live with them full-time.

When I asked him to pack his bags again, I knew that this time it would be for the last time.

BEHIND THE SCENES

Back For Good?

Take a look around the internet and you'll find hundreds of websites with advice and tips of what to do if the opportunity of a reconciliation with your ex-partner or husband presents itself. You can find articles on everything from "what went wrong and why?" through to "how to build the trust with your ex when you don't believe a word he says." When it comes to making such an important decision, what should you really consider before you make your choice?

The urge to get back together with an old partner shouldn't simply be because it's preferable to the prospect of having to start again with someone new or that you are lonely, even if you are! You have to decide if you'd rather stay on your own or face the long process of building back the trust and taking a risk on something that has no guarantee of success.

He may well be missing the children and the familiarity of your old life together but these alone are not good enough reasons for him to want to come back. If you do reconcile, after a while, he will no longer miss them and there will be bigger issues to deal with.

If your ex has come back because it did not work out with your replacement, then that's not reason enough either. It's important for you to know why it didn't work out. For example, if his new girlfriend hadn't ended the relationship, would he still be asking to come back to you? You have to know that you are the first choice, not the second.

Everyone will have an opinion and they will likely want to let you know what you should do. Nicola, who was 30-years-old, had just started to feel like she was getting her life back together when, after nine months, her partner asked to come back. Her friends were horrified at the thought she was even considering trying again and were all saying similar things: *"After what he has put you through?" "He won't be welcome in my house" "Leopards never change their spots."*

Nicola was no longer in that place of anger and started to regret oversharing so many graphic details at the time of the break-up.

On the other side, her family brought a different point of view. *"Maybe you should give it another try. Better the devil you know!"* They reminded her that she would be much better off financially with two working incomes. Her mother was quick to point out, *"It would be different if you didn't have children, but since you do, you should give it another try."*

Despite all the opinions, making a decision on the advice of people who ultimately don't have to deal with the consequences wasn't wise. Nicola knew in her heart that there was only one opinion that really mattered and that was her own.

Affairs of the Heart

If an affair has been the cause of your break-up, it can be helpful to understand a little more about the kinds of affairs, as there are different types. Sexual affairs are driven by physical desire and a lack of emotional intimacy. Emotional affairs are often based on fantasy; rather than meeting in person, the contact takes place by text, email or online. Then there is the full blown love affair which is much like a secondary relationship. It includes sexual contact, friendship, common interests and routines. Affairs are intoxicating, exciting and very addictive. No matter which kind of affair broke up your relationship, there is one common denominator: there has been a breakdown of trust.

Affairs tend to be a sign that something in your relationship had been missing, perhaps something small but important enough for your partner to stray. However that's not always the case. People who are relatively happy in their relationship at home can still have affairs.

Given how complicated affairs can get, it's important for you to have enough details about what happened in your particular case to be able to come to some kind of closure. You need to find a way to stop the constant questions in your head, particularly if you are considering taking him back. It's a good idea to work together with your partner in order to better understand why it happened.

At the end of the day, if you are serious about rebuilding your relationship, you may not be able to do that easily on your own. It can be helpful to call on some professional help to assist in navigating through the many issues and help you both keep things in perspective. Seeking external help is not a quick fix and you will both still need to put the work in.

Is it Really Over?

If there has been an affair, you have to try to make sure that it's actually over and the door has not been left ajar. Unbeknown to one of my 4 o'clock in the morning friends, Lucy, it had been.

When her husband Colin asked if he could come back home after only two months of separation she didn't hesitate to say yes. If they could get everything back to normal as soon as possible she was convinced they would be fine and able to forget everything that had happened in recent months.

She hoped the feeling of constant anxiousness in the pit of her stomach would eventually go away and that the haunting image of her children crying into their cereal bowls at breakfast on the day Colin left, would one day become a distant memory. Colin had told her the affair was over and she didn't want to question it or think of a reason to disbelieve him. She had him back so that was all that mattered.

However, after only a few months after moving back to the family home, Colin admitted that he had never stopped seeing the other woman. When he went on to say that he had made a mistake coming home and was leaving again, the devastation was ten times worse than the first time he had left. She was so angry with him. There she was having to pick herself up again, dust herself off, deal with her disappointed children and then start the healing process all over again. Upon reflection, if she had just taken her time before jumping back in again, she may have saved herself the added heartache.

Life in the Other Camp

If your partner has left you for someone else, you may find that your imagination switches on to overdrive; creating an image of some perfect life that your ex must now be having. You imagine the roses, romance and nights of rampant sex and allow such thoughts to torture you in your alone moments. But what's really going on in the other camp?

Some of what you are imagining might be true; after all, what was it like in the early days you spent together? Yet after a few months (or even weeks) after a partner leaves for another woman, life starts to settle down and sex is interspersed with the daily chores; putting out the rubbish, getting groceries and mowing the lawn. That might be the time that your ex-partner comes to realise that the grass isn't always greener on the other side.

Not only that, it's also quite likely that once the dust settles in his alone moments, he struggles with an emotional reaction of his own; *guilt*. Of course, you may never see any evidence of this, even if you are still in contact with him but guilt is a feeling we all experience. It's an uncomfortable reminder we have done something wrong or hurtful to someone else.

After time, a longing for the old familiar life which he left behind, sprinkled with a little guilt and a massive realisation that he has made a huge mistake, can lead to a swallowing of pride and a courageous plea for you to take him back. For others, pride will take hold and regardless of any regrets, they will stick rigidly to the new choice they made for fear of losing face.

Michael was almost 50, a down-to-earth type of man who worked as a hotel manager for a large hotel chain. He split with his partner Elaine after 18 years together, when he fell for a new recruit who had recently joined his team. At first, he had resisted the flattering attention. He was in a happy and steady relationship and not looking to change that. However, within a few months, what started as meeting for lunch and the occasional drink after work had turned into a full blown love affair.

As pathetic as it sounds, he felt powerless. He still loved Elaine but did he love her *enough*? Surely he couldn't if he had feelings like this for someone else, he reasoned to himself. The stolen moments with his new admirer made him feel alive again but *would it last*? What would everyone say if they found out? He had so many questions but finding the right answers was very difficult when it felt like his head was full of fog. He just couldn't think straight.

When he thought of putting a stop to the affair with his new admirer, he could imagine the look of disappointment on her face and it filled him with dread but the thought of telling Elaine filled him with even more dread. Maybe if he did a fabulous ostrich impression and put his head in the sand, it would somehow all work out the way it was supposed to.

While he was still thinking about what to do, the decision was made for him. Arriving home late after work one evening, he was confronted by Elaine holding his latest mobile phone bill displaying pages of texts to one particular telephone number. The game was up. The following weekend he signed a six-month lease for a rented apartment and immediately moved in his new admirer.

The first few months were not as exciting as Michael had imagined. He quickly realised that stolen moments are very different to living full-time with someone he didn't really know very well. It all felt very odd. He was struggling with excruciating guilt about how he had treated Elaine. After six months, he started to long for his old life and he knew he still loved Elaine. When he decided to go back and ask for another chance, Elaine politely declined his request to return.

No Commitment. No Success

To have a good chance of success in getting back together, it can be helpful to spend time to reflect on the things that previously worked well between the two of you and make a commitment to each other to do more of them. At the same time, it is important to find new ways to do those things that didn't work as well.

It is essential for you both to be fully committed to a reconciliation and want to make it work. You must each be ready to let go of the old relationship you had before the break-up and be open to embrace a new one even though you may not know exactly what that will look like. Letting go is another way of making space to create something new. When we let go of old beliefs, disappointments and expectations, we clear the way for a fresh start.

In the beginning, getting back with your partner may seem as if you have stepped back on the same kind of emotional rollercoaster you experienced in your early days of being on our own. Your emotions can range from relief and joy, to disappointment and frustration and there will be times when you feel you are back walking on eggshells. It's all part of the process.

You may notice that dwelling on the past can bring back the memories of humiliation and rejection. Allow yourself to cry and scream if you need to or laugh out loud, whichever feels most appropriate. If you still feel raw and angry, don't let this stand in the way of a relationship that otherwise would have a good chance of survival. Enjoy the days that are good and go easy on yourself on those days that are not so good.

Are You Ready To Forgive?

Trying again after a betrayal is likely to take hard work. You need transparency, honesty and a lot of communication between the two of you. You must be able to ask the tough questions and hear some truths that maybe unpleasant. More than anything else, you need to be able to forgive.

When your ex-partner has hurt you, it can seem almost impossible to even think about forgiving him. You may try to pay lip service to it but if you are going to have any chance of getting back together, then forgive you must! Even if your ex is not beating down your door, asking to come back and even if you haven't had as much as an apology from him, then forgiveness is still an important step to help you move forward and get on with your life.

You don't have to wait until feelings of hurt and anger have completely subsided in order to forgive someone. You don't have to agree with what they have done or make allowances for their behaviour. You don't even have to see them again or have had an apology from them.

To forgive someone means that you accept the situation and wipe the slate clean of any emotional debt that you feel they might owe you. At the same time, you need to give up your need to have the other person know exactly how much they hurt you.

You need to release any resentment of what happened because holding on to resentment is like holding an ace card in your hand, ready to be played each time you are faced with something difficult. If you let your life fall apart because of something someone else did in the past, it means you aren't in control of your life.

When you do forgive someone, it allows you to let go of the negative energy you have been carrying around with you and supports you to reclaim your power. It gives you space for a fresh start and paves the way for you to act in new ways within all of your relationships, including the relationship you have with yourself.

When it comes to a reconciliation, there are no guarantees that everything will work out exactly the way you hope it will. You will both have changed in the time you lived apart and it's normal that you may now want different things. Your reconciliation may be a hugely empowering experience for one or both of you. It could result in a stronger relationship moving forward or it might just convince you of an undeniable truth; you're just not meant to be a couple after all.

THE REHEARSAL SPACE

Questions. Questions. Questions

When it comes to making a decision about getting back with an ex, there are many things to consider. It has to be the right decision for you and not just the easy one. If you are faced with the chance to reconcile, take some time to reflect on what you truly want before giving an answer. Having had time on your own experiencing a different path, it may not be a relationship that you want anymore. If it is a relationship you would like, it may not be one with your ex.

Take your journal and reflect on the following questions:-
- Why do you want to try again?
- What would be the benefits to you?
- How do you feel about your ex now?
- What changes and compromises are you willing to make in order to move on and rebuild your relationship?
- What are you *not* willing to change or compromise on?
- Will being with this person help you to continue to grow and develop? Will they support you to reach your full potential?
- If your inner wisdom had a voice, what would it say?

Be mindful of what comes up as you answer the questions. If you're still not sure what to do, you might want to talk to someone who you trust and respect to get some more perspective. If your intuition is signalling to you that it's not a good idea, then don't ignore it. In the end, it is your choice so choose wisely.

Learning to Trust Again

Reconciliations provide a chance to make a fresh start so before you begin to invest your time and efforts, try to ensure that you are both equally committed to making it work so you can build a firm foundation together. A big part of a successful reconciliation is finding a way to rebuild the trust.

If there was an affair and you feel like only the full story will do, then ask for it. If there appear to be any gaps in the story, have the courage to ask for the clarity you need. You need to have enough information to settle your mind so you don't end up bombarding your partner for details each time you feel vulnerable.

Agree to have some protected time to talk about the betrayal element of your relationship and set a limit of 20 or 30 minutes at a time so it doesn't consume all your time together. You may need to have several discussions so watch the balance. Make sure it's you that gets to make the decision to reduce the time you spend on talking about it over time.

In the short term, it's reasonable to ask to look at mobile phone entries and emails in order to feel reassured that what your partner says and does is consistent. If he has nothing to hide and it helps you feel assured that he is telling the truth, he will not mind you checking.

Avoid humiliating your partner. You have to decide whether you want revenge or you want a relationship; you can't have both. Step into his shoes to see it from his perspective. If he has admitted making a mistake, which part of that do you not believe? What needs to happen in order for you to forgive him? You will have a greater chance of success if you communicate your concerns in a way that leaves your partner motivated to re-establish the trust.

Keep communicating throughout the early weeks and months of getting back together. Don't distract yourself in order to avoid issues or keep the peace. Instead, commit to addressing any issues head-on together, even if they are uncomfortable. It's natural to have wobbles so use protected time if you need to, in order to convey how you are feeling and to voice the impact things are having on you. Use your journal to write about how you are feeling, so you can make sense of it all. It will help you articulate what you want to say in a rational way.

Rebuilding trust takes time. It is rarely fast and it's a risk for both people but if you can make it work, your relationship could come out much stronger in the end.

CHAPTER 6
Processing the Loss of Your Happily Ever After

"The secret of letting go is knowing that life will give you something better than it's asking you to give up."
- Guy Finlay

RELATIONSHIP REFLECTIONS BY SARAH

It was just over 12 months since Neil had left. He seemed to be well settled into his new relationship and although I can't say I was totally at the stage of fully accepting my situation, I was certainly well on the way.

It was such a relief to have more good days than bad days and it was encouraging to have days I woke up to find it didn't hurt anymore. Yet, while there was evidence of us both moving on, I still felt like there was a tiny part of me that didn't quite feel ready to let go and fully embrace my new life. In an attempt to speed up that final closure process, I decided to get the ball rolling and sort out the legal stuff.

I had never been divorced before so I wasn't quite sure what to expect but having made a career as an administrator, I knew that filling in the paperwork wouldn't be too much of a challenge. Attention to detail was my thing. When the final box on the form was completed, I pressed the computer's spell check function and smiled to see that the only error I had made was spelling of the word "adultery".

What proved to be a much bigger challenge was actually getting to the court offices to submit the paperwork. It took me three attempts. The first attempt had to be abandoned. I had asked a friend to accompany me for moral support in exchange for a glass of wine afterward. An hour before we were due to leave for the courts, she telephoned me and was sobbing profusely. In between the tears, she delivered the awful news that she had lost her job the previous day and was now out of work. We decided to skip the court and go straight for the wine.

The second attempt started off in a more promising way. When I turned up at the court, I was invited to walk through a huge metal detector contraption, similar to those used by airport security. I couldn't understand why my insides and outsides needed to be scanned. It all seemed rather extreme given that all I was there to do was to file divorce papers.

On clearing security I stopped one of the security men to ask where I needed to go to file my divorce paperwork. He gave me a rather odd look, before commenting, "This is the Criminal Court, love. You only need to be here if you've *murdered him*." It appeared I was in the wrong place and needed to go to the Civil Court across town. I was mortified so I abandoned the expedition and rescheduled for the following week.

It was third time lucky. When you are going to hand

over paperwork that will start the process to end your 16-year marriage, you would be forgiven for thinking that it would be more of an event than it actually was. It seemed significant to me but to the lady behind the counter, it was a non-event, I could have been cashing a cheque or taxing my car. The woman did her best to show a bit of empathy as she quickly scanned my paperwork and gave me a receipt. It was just routine to her but I felt rather embarrassed. How come I was feeling this way when I was the innocent party? I felt quite irritable.

With the divorce petition submitted, all I had to do now was wait. It took a few months and filling in some further forms before the large brown envelope arrived on the door mat with the confirmation that my marriage was dissolved.

I sat on the stairs by the front door for about 15 minutes just staring at the decree absolute in my hands. I was now *a divorcee*. In those few moments of reflection, I felt a mixture of emotions but by far the most prominent was a deep sense of failure and shame. I thought about my wedding day and the hopes I had held for the future with a man I loved very much and who up until recently still had. Now it really was over. I remember trying to tell myself it didn't matter and lots of people were divorced but having an official legal document to remind me seemed to make it so much worse. I wondered would it be better in the future if I declared that I was single, rather than admitting that I had once been married but my husband had left me. In hindsight at least being a divorcee proved that someone at one time had loved me enough to marry me. Eventually I put the paperwork back in the envelope and hurriedly filed it away in my life admin box where it still remains today. Out of sight but never out of mind.

BEHIND THE SCENES

The Shame of It All

It seems that regardless of how long ago the break-up was, we can never escape the emotional rollercoaster that accompanies it. As soon as we feel that we have dealt with one upset, something else will be waiting in the wings to try and catch us out. By far one of the most unpleasant of all emotions to deal with is shame. Shame is that feeling that we are not good enough and it makes its grand entrance when we are at our most vulnerable.

When John left me, I was sad. When I found out he had left me for someone else, I felt shame. It is hard to describe what shame feels like but it was too horrid to even acknowledge and made me want to run and hide. I worried that people would think that there was something about me that made me un-loveable. I tried to cover it up by putting on a brave face to the outside world like I wasn't bothered, when inside I was anything but okay.

Many of us attach our own self-worth to our relationship status and it is neither healthy nor helpful so know that just because someone chose not to love you any more, it does not mean that you do not deserve to be loved. You are good enough, just as you are.

Not So Happily Ever After

We all know that most endings don't turn out the way they do in the traditional fairy tales where everyone lives happily ever after. I often think that Cinderella, Snow White and Sleeping Beauty have a lot to answer for; setting our childlike expectations and not quite preparing us for the disappointment that love in the real world can sometimes bring. I wonder how would the Cinderella story have ended if the slipper had fitted several lovely ladies at the ball and not just her? And what really did happen after she ran off from the ball at the stroke of midnight? Did the prince have a quick caress with someone else waiting in the carriage queue?

We never had the pleasure of Cinderella 2 or Snow White the Return to find out what happened years later to these childhood heroines. Maybe their Prince Charming wasn't so charming after all. Who knows? Maybe some of our role models could have found themselves *suddenly single* or facing the divorce courts a few years after their fairy tale weddings. How that would have shattered our dreams!

If we have to deal with endings all the time you might wonder, *why we are not so great at handling them?* What actually is *an ending* and what makes it so tricky to deal with?

Make the Change – Manage the Transition

In our lifetimes we will experience all sorts of endings. Some of these endings will be pleasant and some not-so-pleasant. An ending is the first step in any changing landscape and this brings with it much uncertainty and discomfort. We would much rather have guarantees that everything new or different we face will be successful and work out well but that's not how life works. When it comes to relationships in particular, we tend to hang on tight to the very last remnants; terrified to let go and to acknowledge it has ended.

In his book *Transitions*, American author and speaker William Bridges helps us make sense of endings and unexpected changes in life by helping to explain and normalise the process we find ourselves going through. When we understand more about our change experiences and what is happening to us, we are better able to accept it and move through it without such resistance.

There are two parts to any change. There is the actual change itself. We leave a job and we start a new one. We sell a house and move into a new one. We get married and at some point later on, the relationship might end. Bridges describes this change as external. It's the actual event or circumstance, which is situational and happens in a moment. Change happens to everyone even if we don't agree with it or want it. Change describes the way something will be different.

The second part of the change process is what is known as the *transition*. This is the emotional process that follows what we need to go through in order to deal with the actual change event. Transitions are an internal experience and happen in our minds.

It's interesting to learn from Bridges that *transition* has three stages of its own that can be referred to as: endings and letting go; the neutral zone; and a new beginning.

So to summarise, the actual change event happens quickly and in a moment while *transition* usually happens much more slowly. The time it takes to endure a transition period is different for everyone but each stage is necessary if we want to fully move on. If we don't go through all the stages, it will just be like rearranging the furniture in your home. It's still all there but in a different place and there is no space for anything new.

Endings and Letting Go

Letting go after something ends is the first stage of the transition process. This involves letting go of the past, which is our old identity and who we were in the relationship. For example you were so-and-so's wife, partner or girlfriend and it would be how some people identified you. I was John's live-in partner and fiancée and it's the same for me. It's important that we take time to grieve the loss of that part of us; the identity we held and it's normal to experience the emotions that are familiar to us during any grieving process, such as denial, anger, frustration, sadness, or resentment. No matter how much letting go scares us, it must be done in order to move on. It's the only way to create a space and allow for whatever comes next in our lives.

When we come to accept the loss of identity, an even bigger resistance we face is the fear of the empty space that will be created when we finally let go. Being totally alone creates a void and in that void we are exposed to our deepest primal fears of rejection and abandonment.

Tracey, who is a successful lawyer, was one my first ever coaching clients. When we met she told me that she was feeling "stuck" and wanted some help in moving forwards with her life. In an attempt to hang on to the familiar after her partner of seven years moved out, Tracey had pushed for a platonic relationship and to be "just friends" with her ex, Matt. She was still very much in love with him and the thought of never seeing him again was just too much to bear. There hadn't been anyone else involved in the break-up so she thought that she would be able to manage it. Matt, on the other hand, had been planning his departure for some time so he was much further along accepting the end of the relationship and was back on the dating scene. Yet to ease his own guilt, he agreed to stay in touch.

For Tracey, resetting the relationship back to a casual friendship just stalled the letting go process. She told me that she would sit through their conversations dreading the moment he would talk about something he had planned that didn't involve her and it hurt her deeply. Even though her head said it was over, her heart held on tightly and couldn't seem to let go.

If the end of your intimate relationship was not mutual,

then having an ongoing "friendship" delays the moving-on part of the process and can give you a false sense of comfort and control. The only thing you lose when you let go of something you are afraid to live without is the fear itself.

Entering the Neutral Zone

When we have braved the letting go of the relationship, we enter the "neutral zone". This is when the past has gone but the new reality isn't fully present. It's an unfamiliar landscape, within which you can easily find yourself with one foot in your old world and one in the new. It's like a state of limbo. The old ways don't work anymore and the new ways don't feel right either. The neutral zone is not a very comfortable place, which is why most of us try to rush through this phase of transition.

Within a few months of splitting from her husband, Ruth started to date Frank who she had met on an online dating site. Frank had just recently separated from his wife and was coming to terms with the end of what had been a 13-year marriage.

Within weeks, Ruth announced to all her friends that she had found love again and that she and Frank were making plans for a future together. The romance came to an abrupt end when she asked him to move in. Frank got cold feet from the speed of what was happening and tried to slow things down. Ruth got upset at the perceived rejection and after a big argument, the fledgling relationship came to a rapid end. Upon reflection, she realised that she had been so hung up on her mission to replace what she had lost and stop the loneliness, that she hadn't taken the time she needed to process the original loss of her marriage.

I like to think of the neutral zone like sowing a seed. It

stays underground taking root. From the surface it doesn't look like much is happening but it's a very fertile and important time. In the same way that the seed must wait until the right time before breaking through the soil, we also must deal with a time of nothingness before we are ready to blossom into something new. Existing in the nothingness can bring to mind old fears and all the old fantasies about death and abandonment but it's still necessary to experience. New growth can't take root and take place on ground that is still covered by old habits, attitudes and perspectives.

A New Beginning

The final stage of the transition process is a new beginning. At this point, we have re-adjusted to our situation and our new world and it now feels familiar. We may never feel okay about what happened but we accept it; ready to enjoy life again. At this point, we establish new routines and relationships with others, as a new phase of life finally gets started. Each person who emerges is ready then for a new beginning and will have a different perspective on life.

We can never replace what was lost but interestingly, when we look back, we may come to the conclusion that we actually wouldn't want to. The place we have arrived at in our new life is much better.

Knowing what to expect at each stage in the process helps us make sense of it all and see where we are on the path. Since the timing of each stage is not set, it doesn't matter if it takes us longer or shorter than someone else. At times, we might feel as if we are striding ahead only to hit a wall and retreat back for a short period. The important thing to know is that wherever you are right now, you will get to your new beginning in your own good time. In the meantime, be in each moment and fully live it.

THE REHEARSAL SPACE

The Closing Ceremony

Events of any great significance always finish with a grand closing ceremony. You may not feel that your relationship met the dizzy heights of the Olympic Games but nonetheless, a ritual to mark the ending provides you with an opportunity to acknowledge the past and help you move through the transition process.

Here are some ideas you can use to prepare, plan and hold your own closing ceremony so you can step into your new beginning in an empowering way.

Turn off the TV, switch off your telephone and disconnect from the internet. Have some paper and a pen to hand.
The first step is to set your intent; you are ready to move on. It isn't necessary at this stage to work out the "how" but rather you just need to have a willingness to believe that moving on is a possibility.

Write your intention on a piece of paper. An example could be, "*I am now ready to fully let go and move on.*" Make sure the words resonate with you and have a positive vibe.

Make a list of all the things that you want to let go of relating to your old relationship. Since transition relates to the emotional process of letting go, it's very important to get in touch with any remaining bits of pain or frustration that you feel might still be holding you back.

Give a name to the emotions that you no longer want to feel and include them on your list of things you want to let go of. Disappointment, resentment, anger, or whatever that is for you. It's your ceremony so use any words or pictures that ring true for you.

Now pick a time that is good for you to have your closing

ceremony. It could be early morning, at sunset, or on a particular day of the week. Choose a favourite space in your home where you can create the right environment or somewhere outdoors if that's preferable. Wherever it is, it needs to feel right for you.

Light a candle and read your intention out loud. Then read through the list of things that you no longer want to hold on to. When you come to the end of the list and it's safe to do so, burn the paper or shred it into tiny pieces and dispose of it. Blow out the candle and let it all go.

Releasing the Remnants

Even after your closing ceremony, you will quite likely notice that in the weeks that follow, there are other elements of your past relationship that you are still holding on to. You may have stored text messages or emails from your ex that you haven't deleted and find yourself re-reading. These may require a separate digital closing ceremony of their own.

Find an outdoor space where you like to be. It could be your garden, a park, by the water, or in the countryside, wherever feels right for you. Take out your mobile phone and delete anything you are unnecessarily holding on to. You may need to have an indoor ceremony in the same way if you have stored emails on your computer. It's normal to feel an emptiness inside after pushing "delete" but know this will pass and is part of letting go.

If the t-shirt your partner left behind is acting as a comfort blanket, then put it in the recycling bin and put on one of your own. If photos that are still on display around the house are causing you to reminisce and feel even lonelier, then put them out of sight until you feel ready to decide what to finally do with them.

You don't have to get rid of everything that is connected to the relationship but removing visual reminders of that relationship from your sight is a good first step if you are not yet ready to completely let them go. You can always make a decision as to what to do with them at a later date.

Everyone passes through transition in their own time. Just trust that each small step you make is one more step towards your new beginning.

CHAPTER 7
Discovering Your True New Self

"You only live once, but if you do it right,
once is enough."
- Mae West

RELATIONSHIP REFLECTIONS BY REBECCA

I had been married twice and now I was heading for divorce number two. The ending of my first marriage had been mutual and amicable so I wasn't at all ready for the dreadful sense of pain and betrayal that I had felt this time around. My second husband had left me for a good friend of mine. It was a double loss that left me reeling with heartache for many months.

After my first marriage had ended, I initially embraced my newly single status but not for long. I was young and eager to find a replacement to fill the void that had been created. Before I knew it, I was dating and in the arms of my soon-to-be second husband. Nine years later, that second marriage was over too.

It took me about 18 months before I reached a place of acceptance with what had happened. Every other weekend I would get myself in such a state of anxiousness at the thought of my son spending time with his father and the woman I had once considered a very good friend.

I was exhausted by the amount of energy I was investing in obsessing over the thought of them as a couple and I was further drained from the mental torture that accompanied it. And for what? It was so ludicrous. What I knew to be true was that during those weekends was that my son was in good care, well looked after and he never failed to come back in good spirits.

"*Sometimes you need to be alone to find out who you really are and what you really want in life.*" I saw this quote on a friend's social media page, advertising the services of a life coach. It felt like it had been posted just for me.

A week later, I was sitting in a warm and welcoming office ready to start my first session. I wasn't sure if a life coach was what I needed but from the explanation I had been given during our brief telephone chat a few days earlier, I was willing to give it a try.

My life coach, Vanessa, explained that based on what I had told her, she understood I was looking to get some clarity on who I was and figure out my "*what's next?*" I breathed a sigh of relief to hear that we would be getting perspective on all areas of my life and not just focusing on my failed relationships. Coaching, she went on to say, was a safe place where I was listened to and wouldn't be judged. My answers to her questions were neither right nor wrong, they were just the answers. Her role was to champion me on. I started to feel this was exactly what I had been looking for.

We dived in and started to create a big picture view of my life. I realised I had a lot to be thankful for. There were some things that were working well, particularly when it came to my friends and my relationship with my son. Money was tight yet I was still managing to provide for us both and my ex was contributing in both money and time. This meant I did get some time to myself which, up until recently, I had not been taking advantage of. I was spending too much of that time ruminating over my failed relationship.

I came to realise that when I was "Rebecca the Wife", I had willingly compromised in both of my marriages and somewhere in the process of becoming a wife and mother, I had gotten so used to putting everyone else first, that I had lost myself. When I started to reconnect with long forgotten parts of myself, it became clear there were other important areas of my life that were crying out for attention.

In particular, my career had taken a backseat over the last 18 months. I had taken on an additional role at the local government offices where I worked, but now I was getting bored because it didn't challenge me. Although that had been okay for a while after the split and allowed me to concentrate on simply surviving, I now felt I had the capacity to take on something new.

I agreed to explore some options that would enhance my chances of promotion. When I saw a management training programme advertised at work, I signed up and was delighted to get a place. It was a reminder of how important personal growth was to me and it was fun to rediscover how much I enjoyed the buzz that comes with learning something new. Simply agreeing to that one small action became the catalyst for creating other new opportunities for myself.

I came to thoroughly enjoy time with my coach. I came to respect and admire the new Rebecca who was emerging and felt excited by the life goals that I was setting for myself. I not only had the confidence to make plans for a future of my own but also gained back the hope that it was possible. Who knew that committing to having a relationship with yourself could feel so exhilarating?

BEHIND THE SCENES

A New Beginning for the New You

The great news about tough times is that they don't last forever. It's rather like the seasons. In the dead of winter, we know that spring is on its way. One day we wake up and we can feel it in the air. It suddenly feels different. We look around and see new shoots starting to sprout from the seeds sown, the days feel warmer and the increase in daylight hours make us start to feel lighter and more alive. Spring has arrived and with it, a new beginning.

Being single again brings with it the opportunity for a fresh start. We may have had to let go of the dreams and plans we made with our previous partner but now we have the chance to have dreams of our own and make plans to move towards them. Regardless of your status, it is possible to create a life that is fulfilling rather than one in which you just exist.

When we are faced with a new beginning after coming through a difficult time, it can feel overwhelming. How can you dare to dream big without letting the fear of disappointment get in the way? How do you control the chatter in your mind that stops you even trying? Where do you even begin?

A Relationship with Yourself

It is your life experiences that shape you and cause you to stretch and grow as a person, if you allow them to. Even though you may think that it's just the circumstances in your life that have changed, there will be aspects of yourself that have changed too.

When you begin a new intimate relationship with someone, you want to know all about them. You start with the superficial things such as their interests, their favourite colour and what they like to eat. But what you really want to know is who they are at their core and what is important to them. What do they think? What qualities do they possess? Is honesty important? What are they passionate about? What drives them mad? Where do they limit themselves? Will they be faithful?

When you're part of a couple, you'll spend time investing in the relationship. You will seek to have the other person's best interests at heart. You'll compromise; sometimes willingly and sometimes not so willingly.

Now is the time to invest that same level of energy and interest in developing a relationship with yourself. You can start by asking yourself these big questions: *Who am I? What is important to me now? What is it that I really want for myself given my new situation?*

You have unique talents, life experiences and wisdom, but you might not have given them much thought in recent years. Now you can turn your focus inwards and begin to learn more about who you are, what makes you tick and what's most important to you. It means that every day, no matter what the circumstances, you are heading in a direction that takes you towards a fulfilled future.

Valuing Your Values

A good foundation for developing a fulfilling life starts with becoming clear on your values. Values are like the DNA of your soul. They are not morals and not a sense of what is right or wrong. Neither are they principles like standards of behaviour. A value is something that you believe to be funda-mentally important and your values shape who you are.

When you honour your values and live your life by them, they give you a sense of purpose and make you feel alive. Your values not only motivate you to take action but to take the right action. If you ignore your values or have someone disrespect what you hold as a value, then you are very likely to feel stuck, stressed or frustrated.

Any time you are called upon to make any big life choices or simple everyday decisions, you can use your values to make those choices. Each choice you make, large or small, as long as it is aligned with your values, allows you to move towards a more fulfilled life.

Two of my top values are having the freedom to make my own decisions and making a difference in the lives of others. In the earlier days of my career, I worked for a large corporate bank in a well-paid management role. I liked that job; the people were nice to be around, yet there were aspects of that corporate role that frustrated me. I felt that my life was just passing me by and I had a nagging feeling inside that there must be something more to life than a prestigious position in a successful company.

Around the same time, I went on a personal development course and I was introduced to the concept of values. During one of the many self-discovery exercises, I was encouraged to identify my own values and what was important to me. It felt like a light bulb had been switched on. I realised the reason I was running on empty most of the time at work was because I was seriously compromising my core values.

It took me about six months to work out an escape plan and muster up a bucketful of courage in order to actually resign. It was my first venture into starting my own business and the first time in my life that I had consciously made a choice based on my values.

In the months and years that have followed, that first value-based decision led to many more. I have learned that honouring my values is not a guarantee of happiness and can sometimes mean I have to make difficult choices but ultimately those choices have led me to a life of purpose and one in which I can feel fully alive.

Do Something Daring

As we have already seen, the end of a marriage or relationship brings with it a whole host of new experiences and challenges that you have no control over but are still required to face. Many of them will have involved you stepping out of your comfort zone; experiences that you will not be in a hurry to repeat.

When you start to invest in a relationship with yourself, it can be fun to initiate some new exhilarating experiences of your very own.

American author Elizabeth Gilbert wrote a hugely popular book and memoir called *Eat, Pray, Love,* where she tells how she chose to leave an unhappy marriage and spend a year travelling. She spent four months in Italy eating, three months in India finding her spirituality and she ended her year of self-discovery in Bali looking for balance. For her, solo travelling was the ultimate dream and she took the risk, stepped out of her stable, predictable life and escaped from responsibility for a while.

Your circumstances may not allow for something quite so grand, but there are lots of ways to create new experiences for yourself, regardless of your budget.

Allie was a friend of a friend who was looking for a volunteer who would be willing to give up a couple of hours of her time to help Allie try out some ideas for her new business. When I agreed to help it sounded like a fabulous idea. However, as I was driving over to meet Allie, I started to wonder what on earth I had let myself in for! She had told me she was looking to create an experience that allowed women to celebrate their bodies and I was going to be her first client. I was about to have my very own photo shoot; boudoir-style.

The studio was welcomingly warm and the lighting was soft and subdued. With my hair and make-up complete, it was time to get on with the shoot. After a few warm-up shots, my earlier twinges of self-consciousness and inhibitions disappeared and an hour later Allie called out, "*That's a wrap.*" The experience left me feeling liberated, exhilarated and hugely empowered. It was the most fabulous way to celebrate being a woman and I wanted every woman to have the opportunity of feeling the way I had.

When the photo album arrived in the mail two weeks later, it was beautifully gift-wrapped and finished off with a big black bow. It still remains, to this day, one of the best gifts I have ever given myself.

Step Away From Your Comfort Zone

One of the most common regrets of women who have been through the *suddenly single* experience is that when they look back, they either left it too late or couldn't find the courage to get out of their comfort zones and try some new experiences. It's easy to understand why.

Comfort zones are nice. They keep us safe. They are a place where we have a sense of control and everything feels familiar. A break-up forces us out of our comfort zone and into a place of uncertainty so it makes sense why we would feel some resistance to taking on even more insecurity. However, if we want to grow and experience our lives to the full, then it's essential that we go beyond what is comfortable, every once in a while, to seek out experiences that make us feel alive.

When it comes to taking action, one of the most common

barriers is our own negative self-talk. A bit like our intuition it has a variety of different names; the inner critic; the saboteur; the gremlin. My favourite is the Chimp.

In his best-selling book *The Chimp Paradox*, English psychiatrist Professor Steve Peters refers to the part of the brain that stops us in our tracks when we want to try something new as the Chimp. He describes it as an emotional thinking machine. Its sole purpose is survival and it is designed to keep us safe from any type of perceived danger. It has certain traits and when it comes to us making decisions about the changes we want for ourselves, it gets very nervous. It can think catastrophically, overreact to situations and jump to conclusions; getting things out of perspective when it is faced with uncertainty. It can be our worst enemy but if we learn to recognise and manage it, the Chimp can be our best friend.

Your Chimp will try and talk you out of doing things and it will use any kind of message it needs to. It will tell you that you're no good at that task or hobby. It might say you'll never be skilled in that area, no matter what you do. It might make you feel that the action you want to take is too risky, too expensive, too complicated, too stupid and your Chimp will use any kind of argument to try to put you off. It also can get very bothered about what other people will think about you and the choices you are making.

The first step in managing your Chimp is to simply notice when it tries to hijack your thinking. If you are thinking thoughts that you don't want to think and find yourself worrying, then your Chimp is in the driving seat.

My own Chimp was straight out of its box when I started to think about leaving the corporate world to set up my own business. It was hugely fearful that working for myself would be disastrous and it got me worried about all sorts of things.

The worst was that I would end up with no money if it didn't work out. It then got very catastrophic with a final mantra, "*What if you lose your house?*" Dramatic, I know.

When you are faced with a situation where you want to make a change but you also have to confront such catastrophic "*what ifs*?", the first question to ask yourself is, "*What does my Chimp need to make it feel safe?*" In my case, my Chimp needed a contingency plan so if I did fail I would have a way to pay my mortgage. It was as simple as acknowledging that I could just go back and get a regular 9 to 5 job again if it all went wrong. For added security before I made the change I built a three month reserve of funds in my bank account to allow for any emergencies. It did the trick.

Life actually begins at the end of your comfort zone so whether you are planning for a new experience, such as your first solo holiday or wanting to make a bigger life change such as starting your own business, I highly recommend that you get to know your own Chimp and learn how to manage its negative self-talk. That way, you'll have better success at getting moving and making things happen.

Feel the Fear and Do It Anyway

I would never hesitate to encourage any woman who has become single again to use the opportunity to create a new experience for herself. It doesn't matter what it is, as long as it's something that requires us to step out of our comfort zones and helps us grow in some way. We can sit around and wait for our life to happen or we can go out and *make it happen.* The choice is ours.

It can be inspiring to hear how other women have overcome adversity, learnt something new and stretched themselves to do something different. Over the years, I have coached many women who have been through the *suddenly single* experience in their thirties, forties and fifties. They have managed to find the courage to have a go at something new, that they wouldn't have done if they had still been in their relationship.

Between them they have cycled across India to raise money for cancer; climbed the Sydney Harbour Bridge; changed career to re- train as a nurse; bought a hair salon and started their own business; returned to University to complete a Masters course; ran their first 10km race; picked up a tennis racket after 30 years and joined a local club; and joined a choir and sang at a music festival to an audience of hundreds. These are wonderful women who are living proof that the magic really does begin at the end of your comfort zone.

THE REHEARSAL SPACE

Where Am I Now?

What is important in your life after your break-up may be very different to what was important to you when you were part of a couple. A life of fulfilment in your 20's or 30's and a life of fulfilment in your 40's and 50's are likely to be quite different. It might well be that where you are in your life right now is nowhere near where you want to be.

Take the opportunity to reflect on five important areas of your life: career, personal growth, health, fun and recreation and friendships. You can add another area of your life or substitute one of the suggested five if you wish. Write each of these life categories as headings on the top of a page in your journal and then consider each of the following questions with that category in mind.

- What is your life like right now in this area?
- What are you doing?

- What are you feeling?
- What are you thinking?
- If an observer was watching you, what would they notice?

Once you've written your answers on each of the five or however many pages, then give each category of your life a rating from 1 to 10 that reflects how satisfied you currently are in that part of your life. A rating of 10 means you are totally satisfied and it doesn't get any better and a rating of 1 would mean that you are extremely dissatisfied and need to shout for help.

Now consider that if each area of your life was indeed a perfect 10/10, what would your life look like? What would you be doing, feeling and thinking then? In each case, what is getting in the way? What are the barriers?

The next step is to select just one area in which you want to improve your satisfaction score. Ask yourself, what would be one step you could take which would improve that current score by just one mark right now? You have more chance of success if you take small steps rather than aim to change lots of things all at once. You are not looking to make everything 10 instantly but just to make small changes in each area.

What is Most Important?

Becoming clear about your values and using them to make decisions will always lead to a more fulfilling life. Letting your values be at the centre of your decision-making motivates you to take the right action.

From the following list put a mark beside as many of the words that are important to you. Do this instinctively and do not choose words that you feel you "should" choose. This is your list which means only your values are important. If you notice any of your values are missing then add them in.

- ☐ Achievement
- ☐ Adventure
- ☐ Ambition
- ☐ Boldness
- ☐ Close relationships
- ☐ Collaboration
- ☐ Commitment
- ☐ Competitive
- ☐ Control
- ☐ Cooperation
- ☐ Creativity
- ☐ Dependability
- ☐ Detail
- ☐ Determination
- ☐ Empathy
- ☐ Enthusiasm
- ☐ Equality
- ☐ Faith
- ☐ Family
- ☐ Freedom
- ☐ Fun
- ☐ Generosity
- ☐ Gratitude

- ☐ Harmony
- ☐ Health
- ☐ Helpfulness
- ☐ Helping Society
- ☐ Honesty
- ☐ Humility
- ☐ Independence
- ☐ Inner Peace
- ☐ Integrity
- ☐ Intelligence
- ☐ Legacy
- ☐ Loyalty
- ☐ Making a difference
- ☐ Nature
- ☐ Order
- ☐ Personal Growth
- ☐ Positivity
- ☐ Power
- ☐ Privacy
- ☐ Professionalism
- ☐ Recognition
- ☐ Reliability
- ☐ Reputation

- ☐ **Responsibility**
- ☐ **Results-oriented**
- ☐ Security
- ☐ Self respect
- ☐ Self-control
- ☐ Simplicity
- ☐ Spirituality
- ☐ Spontaneity
- ☐ Stability
- ☐ Time
- ☐ Trustworthiness
- ☐ Truth
- ☐ Wealth
- ☐ Wisdom

Now, looking at all the values you selected, pick the top 10 from your list and see if you can put those 10 in order of highest priority, ranking them from 1 to 10. The ranking of 1 would be your most important. Now reflect on each value. Are you honouring this value in your life right now? What changes might need to happen to ensure that you are honouring this value in the future? Again, think about what decisions you may need to take in order to more closely align yourself with your key values and honour them in your life.

The Best Intentions

When it comes to doing something for ourselves that may be so far out of our comfort zone it seems impossible, then setting an intention is a good first step.

Intentions can assist us in taking greater control of our life and help us to focus our minds on hope and possibility rather than why something is not achievable. They can be especially effective when dealing with tough times.

Simply put, an intention is something that you plan to do. You can set intentions for all kinds of normal everyday things. For example, when I get up each morning, I set an intention on how I intend to be during the day ahead, such as, *"Today I intend to have a productive day."* If you have been struggling with reconnecting with doing the things you love again, which we covered in Chapter 4, then try setting an intention as an initial step.

When we set the intention our minds then start to focus on making it happen.

I invite you to challenge yourself to have a new experience that takes you well outside your comfort zone. The intention is to have an experience that is thrilling, exciting, invigorating or simply makes you gasp.

There are four steps to set an intention and to have the greatest chance of success, all four steps are necessary.

The first step is to get clear about what it is you want. For example, "*I intend to do an abseil and raise money for charity.*" If you have nothing specific in mind at this stage an example might be, "*I intend to create for myself a thrilling experience that takes my breath away.*" Then write it down by hand and have it somewhere so you can view it each day.

For the second step, put a timescale on it. When we use a specific date, it adds a sense of urgency and helps get us into action. If this feels overwhelming, choose a timescale that feels more comfortable (but not too comfortable). So for example, "*I will do this by the end of the summer, within the next three months.*"

The third step is to speak it out loud and then share it with someone you trust and ask for their support. This keeps you accountable.

Then the fourth step is take some action towards it.

When you believe it is possible and take action towards making it happen then the chances are you will not be disappointed.

CHAPTER 8
The Dating Game

"If you are searching for that one person that will change your life, look in the mirror."
-Unknown

RELATIONSHIP REFLECTIONS BY DEBORAH

I had started to become slightly irritated by comments from friends, family or indeed anyone who mentioned they thought it was time I got myself a replacement for my ex husband. I lost count of the number of times I heard, *"Have you got a man in your life yet?"* or *"You are so lovely and I can't understand why you are still single."* Then there was my least favourite from a friend's mother who took every opportunity to tell me that her niece had recently met a man on the internet and after just six weeks of dating, they were making plans to get married. The internet, I was told, was the way to go. Although I knew that they had my best interests at heart, the witty responses I was using to defend my single status were wearing thin.

Heaven forbid that I should go to some social gathering or place on my own. Did people think there was something wrong with me? I had gotten used to going to things alone so why did everyone else seemed to be so bothered? Why did people think that in order to be happy, my life had to revolve around having a man?

I will admit that there were times when having someone to hang out and have fun with did sound appealing. Despite all the heartache I'd been through in the last 18 months, I saw having thoughts about what it might be like to be with someone else as a positive sign. It was a good indicator that I must be doing OK in the healing department. I was certainly getting to like the stronger, wiser part of me that was emerging. I thought that maybe it could be fun to put myself out there and do a bit of dating. I assured my close friends that it was my decision and I wasn't doing it to meet anyone else's needs but my own.

My first hurdle was where to look or go to meet someone. Most of the men that I came in contact with through work were married or had a partner. Now in my late 40s, there didn't seem to be the same opportunities to meet single men as there had been when I was in my 20s; when I had met my husband. With one in three people supposedly divorced, I wondered where they were all hiding.

Internet dating seemed to be the obvious solution. I certainly wasn't looking for someone to marry, just getting out and having some fun would be a good place to start. After thorough market research into the UK's top 10 recommended dating sites, I selected one that gave off more of a friendly vibe than a desperate one.

It was a slow start. My profile was getting viewed and I was more than happy with the flattering description and air brushed pictures that were displayed of myself but I wasn't being inundated with men contacting me. The dating site I had chosen required a friend to write your profile. I figured that way, any man on the site would have had to have at least one friend. I noticed that a lot of the men's profiles were written by the wife of one of their friends, which I found rather interesting and at the same time rather odd.

As I hunted around the site, I compiled a short list of favourites. Some made it to the email exchange stage then just abruptly stopped which I found very rude. Even a "thanks but no thanks" would have been better than a disappearing act and the silent treatment. I quickly learned not to take it personally, though at times it felt quite brutal.

I nearly got to meet two men. Terry from Bolton was very keen until he realised I was 40 miles away and he didn't have money for the diesel for his car. Then there was Roger, who asked if I would reimburse his train fare from Carlisle since it was costing him rather a lot getting around the country meeting women. I was astounded. Is this what dating in the modern world had come to?

Then I met Kenny. After a few emails, we advanced to chatting by phone. He sounded quite nice. He had a distinct tone to his voice and at least he could hold a conversation so I thought that must be a good sign. From his profile, we seemed to have a lot in common and from the photograph, he was quite attractive. We arranged to meet and I found myself rather looking forward to a first date.

I had been standing outside the cafe on the busy main street for about 10 minutes when the taxi pulled up. A rather short, scruffy looking man in tracksuit bottoms, a wrinkled t-shirt and flip flops got out. I was shocked when he walked towards me and said my name. The voice sounded familiar but if this was Kenny, he was nothing like his picture. He smiled to reveal he had no front teeth.

"*It's Kenny*," I heard him say, for the second time. I realised then that I had opened my mouth but no words had come out. Eventually I managed to say, "*You don't look anything like your picture.*" He was quick to explain. "*Oh, that's a picture of my brother. He's much better looking than me.*" If only he knew how true that comment was.

As tempting as it was to get into the taxi that he had just got out of, I felt I should make an effort. We proceeded to sit down and order a coffee but I struggled to find anything that we really had in common. When my friend texted 15 minutes into the date, as we had arranged in advance, to tell me there was "*an emergency I had to attend to at home,*" I made my excuses and left. This wasn't the start I had hoped for but it did help me re-evaluate my expectations and ask some different questions with future potential dates.

As it turned out, internet dating really wasn't for me. Six months later, I met Gary from Glasgow at a charity event through work. I am delighted to report that he had a sparkling personality and all his own teeth.

BEHIND THE SCENES

The Dating Game

When you're going through a painful break-up, the last thing that you are likely to want to think about is dating and meeting someone else. If the break-up has had a particularly traumatic impact on you and healing has been slow and dragged out, then it's easy to understand why you might want to build a fortress around yourself, making yourself unavailable so no one can get near.

However, after spending time getting yourself back on your

feet and starting to feel good about the new you that is emerging, you may arrive at a point when you do start to think about getting out there again to date. If it hasn't crossed your mind, there will be other people only too ready to put the thought in your head.

"*Have you got a boyfriend yet?*" was always the first question I was asked by my friend's 7-year-old daughter each time I went to visit. On one occasion, she and her 9-year-old sister suggested that I may like to watch a TV show with them. It was called *Age Gap Love* and it followed couples who had found love with a partner who was considerably older or younger than they were.

When the credits for the show stopped rolling, the two girls turned to me to see what I thought about their idea to find me love, only to be disappointed to hear that I didn't think that finding a boyfriend would be as simple as the show made it sound.

The world of dating is almost unrecognisable compared to when I was growing up. Back then, you could meet any number of single people at work, out on a Friday night in a local pub or at a nightclub. Now the internet has opened up the options of meeting people from potentially anywhere in the world.

There seems to be a website for every taste. Muddy Matches for those people who have an interest in the more rural type. Uniform Dating attracts people who want to date men or women in uniform, such as armed forces, police or fire fighters. Then there are dating sites that put your friends in charge of your personal profile; to act as a character reference to reassure any interested party that you are the kindest, most honest and funniest person they could ever wish to meet. If all you want is fun, with no commitments and no questions asked, then you can also find that and all only a couple of clicks away.

If you find the online option isn't for you then another choice is speed dating. The dictionary definition sounds mildly terrifying. "*Speed dating - an organised social activity in a private venue in which people seeking romantic relationships can have a series of short conversations with potential partners, one after the other, in order to determine if there is a mutual interest.*"

In a nutshell, you get to meet up to 20 or so allegedly single people, face-to-face, for about five minutes each. It is enough time to check out the chemistry and their conversational skills to help you decide if you would like to meet them again.

The changes on the dating scene mean that there is little left that is taboo. However, there are still some situations that always get a mention. I always wonder why it is seen as perfectly acceptable for an older man to date a woman half his age yet when the roles are reversed and the man is half the woman's age, it still seems to be a topic of conversation. Unbeknown to my friend's two young daughters, I had already discovered that *Age Gap Love* wasn't just for reality TV watchers.

Tom was attractive, kind, extremely witty and 23. At 41, I was older than his sister and younger than his mother so, in his world, that was perfectly acceptable when it came to dating me. We had been introduced through a mutual work colleague who thought we would get on and make a good "plus-one" for each other at a wedding. Our mutual friend didn't really envisage how accurate his prediction would be and neither did we.

What started out as a date at the wedding turned into a summer of adventure, some great conversations and a lot of laughter. It was my first step back into the dating scene and the experience made me feel normal for the first time since my break-up. I never dreamed that it would come from someone whom I could have easily overlooked. By the autumn, the relationship had started to amicably fade and we both went our separate ways though we kept in touch for some years later.

It taught me the importance of staying open and letting go of expectations and going with the flow.

Question Time

No matter which route you take when entering the dating game for the first time after your break-up, it is a courageous step so make sure that you are ready. Before you dip your toe in the water though, there are three important questions to ask yourself.

The first question to pose is, *"What are you looking for?"* If you have an idea of what you are looking for, you have a greater chance of finding it. You might just want to have some fun, meet new people or build your confidence; those are all good reasons to want to date.

Whether you are looking for something casual or someone with the potential to become more serious, then it's important that you look for someone who wants that same thing. It's not a good idea to declare that you are looking for something casual and hooking someone in, when you secretly want more of a commitment.

The second question: *Who are you looking to meet? What type of someone are you looking for?*

Dating is all about getting to know someone and being drawn to someone's profile on a dating site isn't a guarantee that you will feel attracted to them when you meet them face to face.

So while it is useful to have some idea of the type of person that would be a good fit, having a comprehensive check list of what your perfect partner should look like, the job he should have and ensuring his home post code is located in an affluent area can result in a fruitless search. If you are looking for a "Mr. Perfect" you won't find him on the internet or anywhere else for that matter. *People aren't perfect.* They are human so don't have expectations that are impossible for anyone to meet.

Getting out and dating different people is a good way to

determine what a "yes" and a "no" look like for you; what is acceptable to you and what isn't acceptable to you. The type of person you are now looking for may well have changed given your past experience. You have more chance of success focussing on someone who is attractive to you and has qualities and values you feel comfortable with, rather than deciding a potential date on the car they drive.

The third question to ask yourself, "*Are you ready?*" No matter how much you feel you have dealt with your break-up, don't be too surprised if you are still a little raw around the edges. Dating comes with the risk of being rejected. It's part of the territory. Regardless of whether it's been three weeks, three months, or three years since your last major relationship ended, make sure that you feel ready to take the inevitable knock-backs that are part of the game.

If you just want to meet someone to numb the pain of being lonely or to avoid feeling the grief of loss, then you aren't ready. It's not fair to make another person your rebound.

Having considered all that, your next mission, should you choose to accept it, is to decide where to look. Joining a club or group is likely to attract people with common interests and will provide you with opportunities to go out and try different things. It won't necessarily attract other single people, though but you may find that by simply joining a group and being social the need to find someone special is no longer a need.

But on the other hand, if you are really serious about dating, the bigger question to ask yourself is, "*where do single people hang out?*"

The Single Search

With one in five relationships now starting online, meeting someone virtually is one of the most popular ways to get together. If you are considering internet dating, try to remember that online just provides you with the space to meet people. You still have to be careful about who you connect with.

Not everyone online is going to treat you the way you would expect to be treated. You're going to be judged on your picture, not your personality. You are likely to experience people who are not telling the truth. Many will get in touch by email and then after a few interactions, they disappear for no apparent reason. Don't take it personally.

Joanna is a good looking, warm and bubbly brunette so it was a mystery why after 12 months on one of the largest dating sites, she hadn't had a single date. There were plenty of email exchanges, a few which seemed promising but on the suggestion of a meet-up the men disappeared.

Joanna later learned that this was quite a common occurrence. It wasn't the experience she hoped for yet it did encourage her to take her search offline. Some months later, she met an ex-boyfriend at a school reunion and romance returned.

There are plenty of examples of successful romances that do start online, so don't abandon all hope after the first disappointment from the online world.

When the Whistle Blows

If you are like me, then you will generally know within a few minutes of meeting someone, if you would want to spend an evening in conversation with them. If the thought of the online dating option fills you with dread and you are looking for another approach then the world of speed dating may be more to your taste.

The popular Spanish restaurant with its subdued lighting and small tables was the perfect venue to host an evening for single men and women to potentially meet a special someone.

Helen, an attractive, rather shy woman in her mid-forties paid her money to the organiser and was given a table number and a slip of paper. She took a complimentary glass of wine from the bar and was told when she heard the whistle, she should sit at the table number allocated. Her first date would come and make himself known. Helen was fairly confident that after a five minute chat with someone, she would know whether she would want to see him again. It seemed a much better way to meet people than online.

When the first whistle blew, 18 women sat at their numbered table and the 18 men each found their way to their first date of the night. Five minutes later, another whistle signalled that the time was up and the men moved to the next table.

Her assumptions that everyone would be weird or think she was weird turned out to be a story she had made up in her head. On the whole, the men she met had similar expectations as she did as to what the evening would bring. She was pleasantly surprised to find all had the ability to hold a conversation. Helen couldn't remember laughing so much. It all seemed so ridiculous but it was the most fun she had in ages.

Within a few minutes of Date Number 7 sitting down, there was an instant connection and Helen knew she would be more than happy to have a longer conversation with him. He was the one of three to make it to her scorecard. When the whistle blew for the final time, she was so pleased she had made the effort to attend and hadn't let her nervousness talk herself out of it.

The email that arrived two days later contained the contact details of one mutual match. Date Number 7 had obviously felt the same. It signalled the start of what was to become a three year relationship.

It's Just Emotion That's Taking Me Over

Dating is a situation in which, once again, our emotional thinking takes charge. We can jump to conclusions about something we've read or take literally something that someone says to us. We can read into simple situations and we can make assumptions which then disappoint us. We can make decisions before we have all the information. Our thoughts get us thinking that every date is a potential spouse before we've even met them.

Simply recognise when this is happening and what you are telling yourself. Let go of your expectations and the check list and instead, take your time to slowly build a picture of that someone new. Dating should always be a pleasure and never a chore so lighten up, let go and most importantly, have fun.

THE REHEARSAL SPACE

The Right Match

When it comes to stepping back into the dating arena, get clear on what you are looking for and manage your expectations accordingly. A little dalliance and some fun are unlikely to result in a marriage proposal by the end of the night.

Think about dating as a way to share ideas and enjoyable moments with someone. It is a space to allow the other person to be themselves, so you can be comfortable being yourself. It is no more complicated than simply finding someone that you get along with. Attraction is important but limiting yourself to specific physical attributes, such as blonde haired men with blue eyes born on a Wednesday in February, could result in a disappointing search. Dating is the first step to a possible relationship so it is important to have a type of person in mind whilst staying open to other possibilities.

Make a list of the most important qualities and values you are looking for in someone and imagine how you would want that person to make you feel when you are in their company. Here are some of the qualities I like to look for to give you an idea: sense of humour, personable, positive, emotionally available, comfortable in their own skin, healthy lifestyle, attractive to me, friendly and fun to be with.

Getting to know a person and what is important to them will set a good foundation for your relationship, should it proceed from casual dating into a more committed relationship in the future.

You may have some non-negotiable parts of someone's personality or values that you would find difficult to tolerate. For example, if you are a naturally optimistic person, you might well find that being around someone who has persistent pessimistic tendencies would leave you feeling drained. Acting outside of your values to keep a relationship going isn't going to work in the long term.

Fact or Fiction?

Good communication is essential for any type of relationship and particularly true when you are looking to step out into the dating scene. When our emotional thinking takes over, it can result in all sorts of havoc but when we understand our own communication style and that of others then we can start to manage it.

I started to date a man who rarely replied to text messages. When he did, the answers were short and came across as rather terse. The texts left me feeling he wasn't very interested and in my frustration, I told him the impact his texts were having on me. He was mortified. I learned that in his world, unless there was a question in a text message, he assumed that a reply wasn't expected. Anything important I would telephone him. He really only used text messages to confirm arrangements and I used text messages to initiate chat and communicate pleasantries. Once we understood our different communication styles and found a middle ground, normal play resumed.

When we don't have all the information about a situation, we tend to fill in the gaps and make assumptions about what is going on. Adopting a more rational approach, where you can have an honest discussion and gather facts and evidence, will help you reach a more realistic conclusion and keep things in perspective. More importantly, it can keep you from ending a beautiful relationship even before it has begun.

Here is a technique to try when your emotional thinking attempts to take over your communication. Take out your journal and make two columns. Write down the two following headings, one at the top of each column.

- What are the facts?
- What am I making up?

In my case, I would have three entries in the Facts column: Fact 1) I had sent a text. Fact 2) He had read it. Fact 3) I hadn't had a reply.

What I made up in the silence was a long list of assumptions which included: *He must be busy. Is he ignoring me? Have I done something wrong? Is he trying to brush me off? He might have met someone else and doesn't know how to tell me. Maybe he has had an accident. Why am I even bothered?*

To process what is happening in your own situation, write it down and then speak your answers from each column out loud to yourself. Even more effective is when you read it out loud to a trusted friend and have a laugh about it. Humour is a great way to keep your emotions from running wild and allows you to gain a different perspective.

"Date Night" with a Difference

If you have concluded that the dating scene isn't for you right now, there are some alternatives. Ask a friend who has been supporting you through your break-up to go out on a "mate date". Make the effort to do something special. Take them out for lunch or dinner or to see a show at the theatre. If your budgets are tight, then agree to "go halves" or pick some activity that is affordable and fun.

You don't have to wait for anyone else to be available. You can take yourself out on a date. Go to the zoo, visit a museum, or take a tour bus around your home town. Spend the afternoon in a coffee shop or take yourself out for breakfast. Take a Sunday stroll around the park and enjoy a candle lit meal with some delicious food.

It might seem a bit uncomfortable at first but there is just as much value in "me time" as there is in "we time".

CHAPTER 9
The Last Married Man

"Integrity is choosing courage over comfort, choosing what is right over what is fun, fast or easy and choosing to practice our values rather than simply professing them."
- Brene Brown

RELATIONSHIP REFLECTIONS BY ANNIE

It had been a tough four years. The divorce had turned my world upside down and everything was very different after all that, including me. A voluntary redundancy offer at work in the middle of all the chaos enabled me to leave the trappings of the corporate world and step into the world of self-employment in the property sector.

When I look back, my old risk-averse self would have told me it was insane to take such a bold step. I can't say that it had ever been an ambition of mine to work for myself, yet once the opportunity had presented itself, my new inner confidence took charge and I grabbed the chance with both hands.

Over the months that followed I put everything I had into the business. The number of hours I was working didn't seem to matter at first. I loved what I did and it was satisfying to know that the steady flow of clients I was attracting was all because of my hard work.

Yet there were times that I did miss having someone to share my wins and losses with. I hadn't given much thought to being in a relationship again. It crossed my mind at times but I didn't really know what I was looking for anymore. On one level, I felt very fulfilled with my new life, yet in the quiet times when I allowed the loneliness to creep in, it left me wondering if I was missing out by not looking for someone special. The wise part of me thought that was sheer madness; I hardly had time to walk the dog let alone spend time investing in a relationship. So when loneliness would pay a visit, I would immerse myself into my business and push myself even harder to keep going and stay busy.

I had met a few men over the years. I even went on a few dates when I could fit them in. Some of the men were single like me and they appeared to be looking for a relationship. There was Josh who was considerably younger than me. After three months of fun, he ended it after he found love with someone closer to his own age. As a consolation he offered to introduce me to his recently divorced father in an attempt to ease the pain of getting over him, which I politely declined.

Then there was a nice French man who at the beginning seemed very straight forward but after a few months, his workaholic tendencies sabotaged whatever time we had. He said he needed some space to think things through and stopped calling. I wasn't sure what there was to "think through" but I wished him well and let him go.

The men I did meet who really liked me and were single generally made it to about the three or four month stage but just when it felt like we might be progressing to a more serious relationship, I would find a reason to end it. I rationalised that I just didn't have any time.

Then there were the married men. I seemed to be like a magnet for them. Don't get me wrong, I could spot a player a mile off. These men often appeared to be in what seemed like reasonable relationships and yet, on some level, they were searching for something more fulfilling and they thought I was the answer.

Having been on the receiving end of an affair by my husband, I was adamant that dating married men wasn't an option. However, meeting such a man for coffee or a drink to determine if he was available seemed to be a sensible initial screening process. After all I didn't want to miss an opportunity and thought I might find someone with mitigating circumstances. The reality was I didn't and after a few encounters, I would end up walking away leaving the man to return home faithfully with his family-man-reputation still intact.

Then I met Alex. His situation seemed very different. He was living in the family home with his wife and youngest daughter but they appeared to be leading separate lives. No shared interests, little time spent together and separate bedrooms. In his words, it was a 25-year amicable relationship in which his daughter was the glue that had kept him and his wife together. His longer term plan was to stay until his daughter left home to start university and then they could go their separate ways. This was 18 months away and until then he had a responsibility to his family. He was very clear that his situation would not be changing.

At first I was naturally suspicious of his account but over the months, as our friendship grew, I started to let my guard down. Alex was the most delightful man, very kind with a huge capacity to love. We had a lot of quality time together and he was quite happy to work around my business commitments. His whereabouts were never challenged and he was never questioned as to where he had been on the nights that he never made it home.

When he was happy to meet my friends and family, I assumed that his intentions about me must be serious. When they all told me that they thought he was great it was the permission I needed to let down my barrier completely. Yet as much as they liked him, they were quick to question that if he really was serious about me, what was stopping him telling his family? If he was leading a separate life to his wife, as he obviously seemed to be, why was he not being honest about seeing me? Didn't his wife have the right to know? His daughter was a young adult. Why not sort out his situation now? His intended plans would mean that I would have to wait and they knew me well enough to know I wasn't keen about putting my life on hold for a promise that might never happen.

I knew in my heart they were right and that I should let him go but after you've spent many an evening home alone with your favourite DVD box set and a glass of wine and then you have the option of male company and intellectual conversation with someone you are attracted to, someone you could perhaps see yourself being with, this was hard to resist. So for 12 months, I didn't resist. Instead I chose to ignore the dissonance in the pit of my stomach and compromise my value of integrity, all the while convincing myself that it would all work out just fine.

However, as the months passed, the idea that I was being kept a secret quietly gnawed away at my insides. I didn't want him to leave his situation, I understood it, but I did want him to acknowledge my existence. Surely we could all sit down and work things out? In my world, it was the honest thing to do. Yet in his world, he did not think it was necessary.

A brave friend wondered had I noticed that when he had a family commitment and he and I had already made plans, it was always the family commitment that took precedence. My busy work schedule had been masking the reality. When he unexpectedly announced that he was going on a family holiday for a month and would see me when he got back, my inner instincts shouted "enough" and I acted upon its wise advice. It was time to let him go.

It was a most painful lesson and one I am thankful I will never have to learn again. *Alex was to be my very last "unavailable" man.*

BEHIND THE SCENES

Four Stages of Dating

So you have dabbled in a bit of dating and have met someone whom you kind of like but when the relationship feels like it's ready to move forward, you try to stall and put on the brakes. You are confident this new love interest isn't an axe murderer and is possibly someone you could see yourself being with, yet despite your instincts indicating it's safe to proceed, it feels like there is a barrier that is stopping you and you can't seem to break through it. The comments from friends and family might now be suggesting that you're too choosy. But are you really or could there be something else going on?

Just like any other life change, the transition from dating to being part of a committed couple consists of a number of stages. Different models present these kind of stages in various ways, but I like to think that there are four main stages people go through. Similar to the stages of the grief cycle, every part of the process takes each individual varying amounts of time to go through.

Dating is Stage 1 which we have already touched on in the last chapter. If there is mutual attraction and enough interest, you will move into Stage 2. In this stage things still aren't too serious. You are both showing your best qualities and starting to find out about each other. You are likely to be taking your time and not making any hurried decisions.

Once you enter Stage 3, your hormones will be calming down and reality starts to set in. You start to notice differences and so will your partner. So for example his tidiness and your disorganisation might start to create minor irritations that weren't an issue in the early days. In Stage 3, the relationship starts to feel like it's on a different footing and there comes a point when the "Where are we heading?" question can no longer be ignored.

Stage 4 is the final stage, when both people are comfortable having open and honest conversations. They have a good understanding about their own values and those of their partner. If you and your partner have reached this stage, you feel able to handle your differences, let your guards down, open yourselves up to being vulnerable and start to trust each other enough to fully commit to the relationship.

The Heart Protector

There can be a hundred different reasons why we put up barriers to stop from moving toward a committed relationship again. Letting love in involves taking the risk of getting hurt again. If you have loved deeply and had a particularly difficult break-up, then letting your guard down can be a real stumbling block. This was certainly the case for me. For about a year after John left, I must have told myself every day that I never again wanted to feel that kind of pain and emptiness again.

With the passing of time, my heart healed yet when it came to attempting a relationship with someone else, the subconscious mantra that had played over and over in my mind in those early days had become my heart protector. I seemed to attract men who seemed available but actually weren't. If they were available then it wouldn't be long before I had sent them packing.

At the time, I had no idea why I rarely got past the six-month mark. Then one day a friend asked me if I had ever considered that I might be the one who was emotionally unavailable. I had no idea what that really meant but the embarrassed squirm that I felt inside seemed to suggest she may be right.

There are times in life when making ourselves *emotionally unavailable* makes sense. For example, you might do this in the early days after a break-up when it is helpful to have time alone to deal with the loss. Or there might be occasions when you just want to casually date and are not looking for a long term commitment or perhaps you might feel the need to spend some more time focusing on yourself again. These are all choices that you are making consciously.

For anyone who has faced some sort of relationship trauma, such as a painful break-up, being *emotionally unavailable* can be useful as a coping strategy and one which we unconsciously use as a barrier to stop from getting hurt. We can feel ready to embrace life again and want to find a special relationship. We can go through the motions by saying and doing all the right things. Yet the reality is we attract people into our lives that are unable to commit and therefore not able to give us the very thing that we are seeking.

So how do you know if you are *emotionally unavailable* and what are the signs? "You won't marry my Dad, will you?" was the question I was asked one day by an inquisitive 8-year-old. I had been dating his father for about six months. Curious as to what he was witnessing to prompt such a strange comment, I asked why he would think that. His simple response, "Because you are always working."

If you want a relationship you have to make the time to invest in it. Being rigid and not wanting to compromise, making excuses about spending time together and not being inconvenienced at any cost can all be indications that you are not ready or willing to invest in it. If you aren't careful, this behaviour can also spill over into other personal relationships and you could be in danger of isolating yourself from everyone. When I first started my business, I was pleased to meet many other single female entrepreneurs who also had a similar story to tell as mine. It was hugely inspiring to realise how many had faced heartbreak and had directed all their energies into running successful enterprises, just as I had.

Yet at the same time I also had many conversations at a deeper level that revealed what was going on behind the scenes. Loneliness made a regular appearance in the down time. For some it was just an unpleasant side effect of being single that left little impact. Having meaningful work that fulfilled them was enough. For others, there was a fear that stepping forward to invest time in a relationship could result in negative consequences for their business. No matter how wonderful any prospective partner might appear, just the thought of going through it all again, investing in an intimate relationship only to have it not work out was just too much of a risk. It was much easier to protect their hearts and have a relationship with their business or career rather than with another person.

Like Attracts Like

Rather like the season, reason, or lifetime friend that I mentioned earlier in the book, every relationship that comes into our life comes to teach us a lesson about some aspect of our self. *The Secret* is a best-selling self-help book written by Australian television writer and producer, Rhonda Byrne, based on the law of attraction. Simply put, the law of attraction is the ability to attract into our lives whatever we are focusing on. So we are rather like human magnets we send out our thoughts and emotions and attract back more of what we have put out.

Whether you believe the concept or not, it is an interesting thought for which I could produce a number of real life examples that would have the biggest cynic curious to know more. Given this notion, it won't be a surprise for you to learn that if people are emotionally unavailable, it is likely that they will attract others to their lives who are also emotionally unavailable.

There are some very obvious signs that someone else is emotionally unavailable, so obvious you may wonder why you would miss them. I often wonder do we really miss them or rather do we *conveniently choose* to overlook them?

If you are looking for a committed relationship, a person who is married or still in love with someone else isn't emotionally available and ultimately is not going to be there for you. If you do get involved with someone in this situation, you can end up feeling lonely, rejected, disappointed and frustrated and not able to get close to someone you love. Getting hooked on someone who is unavailable is a distraction from the heart of the problem, which in fact is much more likely to be your own unavailability.

Katherine was a smart and single-minded business development director in her late thirties and had carved out a successful career in the media. Five years earlier Katherine had been engaged to be married and at the last minute, her fiancée had a change of heart and called it off. Since then there had never really been anyone else.

Then she met Rick. The first time he walked into her office, the chemistry was overpowering and Katherine was smitten. Whenever she was in his company, everything just felt right and he told her it was the same for him. What she didn't know was that it also felt just right when Rick was with his wife and their two small children.

Katherine refused to acknowledge his situation. She stopped asking him questions about his life at home or anything about his family because the reality was just too painful to hear. It was much easier to block out the reality and hold on to the stolen moments they had together. She reasoned with herself, *If something felt so right, surely it was meant to be.* She found herself acting out of character, making compromises to her work commitments which she would never have done for anyone else, in order to accommodate Rick's busy schedule so she could see him. If her texts, emails and calls were ignored, she could always reason with herself why that would be. She did not care that she was making all the effort. She just needed to ensure that she had done anything to give the relationship a chance.

After three years of waiting and promises that "one day" they would be together, Rick's wife got pregnant with their third child. Katherine realised that unless it was an immaculate conception, Rick hadn't been telling the whole truth about his loveless marriage. When he ended the affair, she was left to deal with the loss of something she had never really had.

Know Your Limits

When you have been single for a while in your new world, it's easy to forget that men you meet who are married or have a partner are not single. They are in a very different situation and they have a commitment to someone else and other responsibilities to take into consideration, no matter how much they protest or try to package it up or explain it away. The playing field is not level. For them to commit to you, it will be necessary for them to make some considerable changes and potentially cause pain to people who love them.

Yes, sometimes people fall in love with other people and leave marriages. You may well have been on the receiving end and experienced that first hand. Yes, it is possible to separate with love and integrity but it is rare that any break-up that is not completely transparent to all parties will escape any sort of drama or frustration.

The message that comes loud and clear from any *suddenly single* women who have found themselves embroiled with someone who is otherwise attached is that, *"Married is messy!"*

No matter how much the person seems to be perfect for you, if that person is emotionally unavailable then there will be limitations. If that's acceptable to you and your values then you will need to manage your own expectations accordingly. If your actions are compromising your values, the result will always be inner conflict.

You have no control over another person's choices but you do have a choice about *what you do.* If you meet someone who is emotionally unavailable, then you can choose to stay and wait. You don't have to give up on someone because their situation is not ideal. All great relationships have problems but they are *great* relationships because both people care enough about the other person to find a way to make it work. If you trust them enough then you have nothing to worry about. However, putting your life on hold for someone who is doing a lot of thinking and talking about their situation and showing little signs of action could result in a long wait.

A great relationship is one that comes easily and naturally. It is a relationship in which two individuals bring out the best in each other and accept each other just as they are. Each person is able to function perfectly fine on his or her own without being dependent on the other. It shouldn't feel like a one-sided uphill struggle all on your part.

We all deserve to have someone of our own who is committed to us fully and completely. You don't have to settle for less or resign yourself to become someone's *secret.*

THE REHEARSAL SPACE

Risk Assess Your Relationships

Learning to trust again after being hurt can sometimes seem like an impossible challenge. No matter what you experienced in your previous break-ups, even if it went fairly smoothly, there are still likely to be scars. When you enter a new relationship and open yourself to love again, it means taking a risk. With any risk, there are no guarantees.

However, to some extent risk can be managed. You don't have to blindly jump in and cross your fingers and toes hoping it will all work out.

Take some time now for reflection. First, think about what you have learned from your past relationships and note down what things you want to do differently moving forward. So for example I learnt to always take my time in that first phase of dating and not rush things. It gave me time to get to know someone and equally important for them to get to know me. Be confident that your instincts will always alert you if something is amiss so you'll be able to act on any early warning signs in a proactive way. Having been through the experience previously, you are much better equipped to know what you are looking for.

Work out what your boundaries are as to what is acceptable and not acceptable behaviour, right from the beginning. This doesn't mean putting up even more barriers or issuing a set of strict instructions or ultimatums for the other person. It is about being sensible and saying "no" to situations that are not acceptable. It also includes saying "no" to people who might not be available right now, for whatever reason.

Look back on the list of qualities that you started to make as part of The Rehearsal Space in the previous chapter. You may find that you need to add more to this list or clarify some of them a little more, now that you might be moving into a more serious relationship.

Again, don't rush in too quickly. Take your time to get to know someone. You want someone who is honest and whom you can trust, but trust takes time to build.

What would you expect to see a new partner do if they were being trustworthy and honest? Remember that you never have to settle for anything less than someone who is going to enhance your life and enable you to be all that you can be and more.

Unhooking Yourself From an Unavailable

If you have gotten yourself hooked in with a man who is in some way emotionally unavailable, the first question to ask yourself, "Is this relationship good for me?"

If the answer is "no" here are a few tips to help you get unhooked.

Be honest with yourself and don't try to shy away from the reality. If he is in a relationship with someone else acknowledge it to yourself. How does that sit with your values?

Make a decision and stick to it. If you are struggling to get the words out, write it down to articulate what you have to say. Like giving any bad news, keep it short and say it straight.

Cut off all contact. You have to go cold turkey for any chance of success, so even if you don't really mean it, ask him not to contact you. If you need to delete his contact details to help you from being tempted, then do so. Make it a priority.

There is no avoiding the fact that such relationships are extra tough to walk away from and it will hurt but it is far better to be sad rather than sad and frustrated. Be prepared to face a sense of loss and rejection, despite the fact that it is you who has made the decision. You have faced it before and survived and you will be okay.

The Right Relationship for the New You

Relationships come in all shapes and sizes. If you want to let love in again, it is likely that there are certain aspects of a relationship that you are looking for now that are very different from the one you let go of. If you are living alone, you may not want to share your space in a permanent arrangement with anyone right now. You may not be willing to compromise your new-found freedom and flexibility and that's okay.

The important thing here is to be clear about what you do want (and don't want) at this particular time so you won't end up in a new relationship that doesn't fit with you and the new life you have created.

In order to become clear on your current needs and wants, take out your journal and reflect on the following questions.

- What would a great relationship look like now?
- What am I hoping that this next relationship will give me?
- What would I have to compromise by committing to a relationship?
- What would be the impact on my values?
- What would be the benefits of a relationship versus being single? Is this enough anymore?

CHAPTER 10
Stronger, Smarter and Simply Fabulous

"Happiness is letting go of what you think your life is supposed to look like and celebrating everything that it is."
- Mandy Hale

MY OWN RELATIONSHIP REFLECTIONS

It has been 14 years since I found that single ticket to the charity ball in the fruit bowl. Of course I had no idea that the painful ending it brought about was actually the start of a new beginning. If someone had even dared to suggest the possibility at the time, when I was hurting so much, I wouldn't have wanted to accept it. Yet that's exactly what it was and what followed turned out to be a significant and transformational stage of my life and one in which I was to discover who I really was and what I was capable of.

At the start of that journey, it felt as if everything had been taken away. My heart and my life had been smashed into so many pieces that I wasn't even sure where to start when it came to putting them all back together. It was like a mammoth jig-saw puzzle. Some of the pieces were familiar and slotted back in quite nicely while others no longer seemed to fit. I was also to discover many new pieces which took quite a while to figure out how to integrate them into my new life. At the time, I didn't have a picture on the front of the box of the new life I wanted to create for myself. I was working that out as I went. All I knew was the life that was unfolding was a very different landscape from the old life I once had and through the process, I was changing too.

Tony was one of my first coach mentors when I started my coach training. I remember talking to him and telling him about a feeling I had of being almost complete. I used my anal-ogy of the jigsaw to explain how over the years, it felt like I had been putting myself back together and a quite different "Denise" was emerging, compared to the one from those earlier years. I had developed more self-awareness, had more resilience, con-fidence and inner strength and it felt very mature. I had learnt to forgive and also I had accepted responsibility for what could have potentially been my part in the break-up. I had worked out what was important to *me*, rather than worrying what about was important to everyone else and this led me to make choices for my life that were more fulfilling than I thought possible.

I told Tony that I felt like I was almost there on the healing front and life was good yet I still felt like inside me, there was still a tiny piece missing inside me. I was coming to the conclusion that maybe I needed to look outside toward another relationship to fill the gap until Tony shared with me some words of wisdom: "If you put your life on hold waiting for someone to come along and make you complete, you could be waiting a long time. What if the missing piece could only come from *yourself*?" And of course, he was absolutely right. I had a little more healing to go.

BEHIND THE SCENES

Taking Responsibility

When we enter a relationship, we have a picture in our heads of the way we want it to be. When our hopes and dreams are shattered or it doesn't work out the way we wanted and we don't get the *happy ever after* we had hoped for, it can be devastating.

To love means taking a risk. We don't have any control over other people's feelings or what they may or may not do, no matter how long we have been together. The only control we do have is a choice on how we deal with what is being presented to us. So when a relationship ends we can choose to lie down and become a victim or we can own our experience and allow the learning to help us grow and create our self a *new happy ever after*. The choice is all ours.

If we let our life fall apart because of something someone else did, we are choosing to let it all fall apart. Not so nice stuff happens, it is part of the ebb and flow of life but by choosing the approach we take, how we respond and how we manage our emotions and thoughts, we can gain a sense of control.

It may take us some time before we are in a position when we feel able to look back on the relationship that left us heart-broken and take responsibility for our part in the split. When I look back and consider my role in the break-up of my relation-ship with John, I do accept that for the 12 months prior to his leaving, I was busy building a business. This left me with little time to invest in our relationship.

He had asked me many times during those months to move away from the laptop and spend some time with him. Different times, he had tried to arrange an evening out but more often than not my response was, "I just need to finish this." I had taken my eye off the ball and someone else had picked it up.

I'm not saying this was a good enough reason for him to seek out comfort in the arms of another person. *Not at all.* I thought that our relationship was strong enough to take such challenges especially as he had totally supported me when it came to my business, but I was wrong.

If I am honest with myself, it does seem like my preoccupation with work was a contributory factor. I did get the opportunity to ask him about this some years later and he said it was not. He had not been unhappy, he had just fallen in love with someone else. I guess I never will know for sure.

The bottom line however is that I chose to spend time with my business, the same way as he chose to have an affair. We are all free to make choices but it also means we have to accept the consequences of those choices too.

Shared Learning of the Suddenly Singles

Thankfully the definition of success when it comes to a great love story is no longer defined by two people walking off into the sunset and living happily ever after. Some great love stories end up with just one person walking off into the sunset and creating themselves an alternative *happy ever after*, one in which they are just as fulfilled and content single, as they would be as part of a couple.

When I went through my *suddenly single* experience, I didn't have a manual with instructions as to what to expect on the road ahead. I faced many road blocks and had to deal with them as best I could. I only wished at the time that I knew that it was all normal.

The learning that has emerged from my own experience and the women whose stories I have shared, I hope will provide a valuable guide to support others, who are having to put the pieces of their broken heart back together and navigate through a new world.

Our collective wisdom offers a set of guiding principles which are not just helpful when it comes to relationships but beneficial in all areas of our lives. All we need to do is let the wisdom in.

1. Learn to listen and trust your instincts, they won't let you down.
2. Have the courage to ask the questions that you may not want to hear the answers to.
3. Take time every day to be grateful. Focus on what you have got and not what you haven't got.
4. Take time to invest in your own self-care.
5. Acknowledge your emotions and let the sadness flow. Tears are better "out" than "in".
6. The healing process won't be hurried. There is no quick fix when it comes to loss.
7. Create yourself a SOS contingency plan to cover any practical areas in life where you feel most vulnerable.
8. Just because someone chooses not to love you, doesn't mean that you are un-loveable.
9. True friends will be there for you and some friendships may not survive.
10. Asking for help is a sign of courage not weakness.
11. Forgiveness is absolutely necessary if you are to move on in your life.
12. Unrealistic expectations of others often leads to disappointment.
13. Whether you are building trust or rebuilding trust, both take time.
14. There is no guarantee of success in any relationship.
15. Set yourself boundaries and be clear what is acceptable

to you and what is not acceptable. It is OK to say "no".

16. You never have to be anyone's secret.
17. There is no need to explain to anyone why you are single.
18. Getting clear about your values and what is important, then create a life that honours them.
19. Step outside your comfort zone to have a new experience. It is where the magic happens.
20. Relationships come in all shapes and sizes but the most exciting, important and challenging relationship you will ever have in life is the one you have with *yourself.*

And Finally...

A woman whom I have gotten to know recently told me that I had the life she wanted. Curious as to what prompted her comment, I asked her to enlighten me. It seemed that her 15-year marriage that looked just like any other marriage to people on the outside was in fact a very different experience for the two people in it. She was with a man she no longer loved and who no longer loved her. She was terribly lonely and felt trapped.

When I asked her why she was choosing to stay in the relationship, she told me that she thought about leaving every day but she was attached to the lifestyle the relationship had created. If she walked away she would lose the house she loved, have to face the inevitable changes to her social circle and ultimately didn't want to be on her own.

Even when I gently pointed out to her that she was already *alone*, she insisted that the fear of making such a drastic change was just too much. What would people think of her if she left? She finished the conversation by telling me that it was alright for me because I was a strong, independent woman. I wondered if she had met me 14 years previously would she still have had the same opinion.

For many of the women mentioned in this book, becoming *suddenly single* wasn't an option. We were merely parachuted into an alien world and had to work out how to create a new life for ourselves while at the same time mend our broken hearts. For other women they chose to stop betraying themselves and made the courageous choice to leave a relationship that no longer served them. Yet they still had many of the same obstacles to face.

The good news is we made it through and we are normal. Some of the women have found love again in relationships that look similar to the one they had been in. Others have found love and created relationships that are very different. Others have embraced being single and are living their life to the full.

And me? Well, I have created a great relationship with myself. I have chosen to live a life guided by intuition and my values. I have discovered who I am and what I am capable of. The love in my life comes from my friends and family. I did fall in love again, but this time when it didn't work out, my heart was bruised not broken. Sometimes I get lonely and sometimes life is tough, but it is always fulfilling and I know that whatever I face that I am good enough. I have found my own purpose in life and now through my work, I help other women find theirs.

Sometimes in life, the *happy ever after* we think we want actually ends up looking very different. As you go forward from here, remember that you are in charge of creating the life you want. My heartfelt wish for you is that you take every opportunity to create the *happy ever after* that suits the fabulous you that you truly are.

Made in the USA
Charleston, SC
27 February 2017